You, _____,
by following these concepts will be able to experience success
God's way, which is the best way!

GOD'S WAY
Is Still the
BEST WAY

GOD'S WAY
Is Still the
BEST WAY

ZIG ZIGLAR

THOMAS NELSON
Since 1798

NASHVILLE   DALLAS   MEXICO CITY   RIO DE JANEIRO   BEIJING

© 2007 by Zig Ziglar

Published in Nashville, Tennessee, by Thomas Nelson. Thomas Nelson is a trademark of Thomas Nelson, Inc.

Thomas Nelson, Inc. titles may be purchased in bulk for educational, business, fund-raising, or sales promotional use. For information, please e-mail SpecialMarkets@ThomasNelson.com.

Unless otherwise noted, Scripture quotations are taken from the New American Standard Bible®, © 1960, 1962, 1963, 1968, 1971, 1972, 1973, 1975, 1977, 1995 by The Lockman Foundation. Used by permission.

Scripture quotations marked NIV are from the Holy Bible, NEW INTERNATIONAL VERSION®. © 1973, 1978, 1984 by International Bible Society. Used by permission of Zondervan. All rights reserved.

Scripture quotations marked TLB are from *The Living Bible,* © 1971, 1997. Used by permission of Tyndale House Publishers, Inc., Wheaton, Illinois 60189. All rights reserved.

Scripture quotations marked NKJV are from the New King James Version®. © 1982 by Thomas Nelson, Inc. Used by permission. All rights reserved.

Published in association with Yates & Yates, LLP, Attorneys and Literary Agents, Orange, California.

Library of Congress Cataloging-in-Publication Data

Ziglar, Zig.
  God's way is still the best way / Zig Ziglar.
    p. cm.
  Includes bibliographical references.
  ISBN 978-0-8499-1963-3 (hardcover)
  ISBN 978 0 7852 8946 3 (IE)
  1. Christian biography. 2. Christian life. 3. Apologetics. I. Title.
  BR1700.3.Z54 2007
  248.4—dc22   2007028846

Printed in the United States of America
07 08 09 10 11 QW 9 8 7 6 5 4 3 2 1

CONTENTS

Foreword by John Maxwell   ix

Introduction   xi

PART ONE: THE INWARD FRUIT OF THE SPIRIT

CHAPTER 1 — LOVE   3
Truett Cathy   4
John J. Eagan   8

CHAPTER 2 — JOY   13
Brian Buffini   14
Jim and Naomi Rhode   22

CHAPTER 3 — PEACE   27
Dr. Dick Furman   28
Wayne Alderson   34
Dr. Leslie Holmes   39

PART TWO: THE OUTWARD FRUIT OF THE SPIRIT

CHAPTER 4 — PATIENCE   47
John McKissick   48
Tony Evans   55
Jim Dawson   60

CHAPTER 5 — KINDNESS   67
Kenneth H. Cooper   69
Gary and Diane Heavin   73
Mary Kay Ash   77

CONTENTS

CHAPTER 6—GOODNESS   79
Butch Davis   80
Mary Crowley   84
Jim Norman   88

PART THREE: THE UPWARD FRUIT OF THE SPIRIT

CHAPTER 7—FAITHFULNESS   95
Bill Bright   96
Mike Godwin   98
Tom Harken   104

CHAPTER 8—GENTLENESS   109
Albert Black   110
Bob Lightner   117

CHAPTER 9—SELF-CONTROL   121
Dave Curry   122
Bill Costas   126
Dr. Ben Carson   131

PART FOUR: YOU WILL KNOW THEM BY THEIR FRUIT

CHAPTER 10—AN INTIMATE RELATIONSHIP   137
Amey "Sunshine" Fair   139

CHAPTER 11—SHARING CHRIST WITH OTHERS   147

Appendix: *Why Must We Be Born Again?*   159
Acknowledgments   161
Notes   163
About the Author   167

To Julie Ziglar Norman,
my youngest daughter and the best editor—the hardest
working and most fun—I have ever worked with.
It's been a delightful experience.
Thank you, Julie.

FOREWORD

BY JOHN MAXWELL

In 1974, my father, brother-in-law, and I attended a conference in Dayton, Ohio. Thousands of people packed the place to hear some of America's greatest speakers. That day, some impressed me—but one impacted me. Zig Ziglar connected with the audience in a way that I will never forget. He charmed his way into the hearts of the people with his humor, insights, and ideas. But his expressed faith in God is what warmed my heart. With great skill and experience, Zig continually brought God into his success story. That night I stood in line for an hour to meet him and walked away with an autographed copy of *See You at the Top*.[1]

Thirty years later, I can say that Zig's enthusiasm for God still warms my heart. We have spoken together on platforms across America, worshiped God together, encouraged each other on some of our country's finest golf courses, and shared many intimate conversations during dinner. I have been beside Zig during his greatest moments and in his darkest hours, and his faith in God has always been stellar. *God's Way Is Still the Best Way* is more than a title for his book; it is the story of his life.

When I was senior pastor of Skyline Wesleyan Church in Lemon Grove, California, our church wanted to have an outreach event for the business community of San Diego. We invited Zig to be our speaker, and more than twenty-five hundred people attended the event. Once again, Zig connected with the audience and shared the gospel with them. That night, many people began their journey with God. That night, I began my journey to learn how to bring Christ to the business community.

God's Way Is Still the Best Way has influenced me to integrate my faith in the marketplace to honor God and to be a witness to those who do not know God. After reading this book, it is my joy to share the following thoughts with you.

First, *this book encourages Christians.* Anyone who is familiar with Zig Ziglar will not be surprised at that statement. Encouragement is the oxygen of the soul, and Zig continually breathes affirmation into the lives of thousands of people, including me. His stories of Christians who are putting God's way to work will put wind beneath your wings. How these people conduct their lives with character will put steel in your soul. The way they creatively share their faith will stimulate your mind.

Second, *this book encourages Christians to live spiritually attractive lives.* I am privileged to know some of the people who are highlighted in this book. They daily exhibit the fruit of the Spirit and model for us how to apply Jesus's command to "let your light shine before men in such a way that they may see your good works, and glorify your Father in heaven" (Matthew 5:16). Their stories will encourage you to show and tell others that *God's Way Is Still the Best Way.*

Third, *this book encourages Christians to share their faith with others.* For too long Christians have kept quiet outside the church and home. This book is full of stories of real people who share Jesus simply and effectively every day—wherever they happen to be. And the final chapter details several practical and simple ways you, too, can let your light shine to others every day.

My friend Zig Ziglar loves the old song that says, "Take the name of Jesus with you . . . Take it then, where'er you go." It is our prayer that when you finish this inspiring book, you will take the name of Jesus with you wherever you go. As you do, lives will be changed and you will say along with our friend Zig, "God's way is still the best way!"

INTRODUCTION

You may have noticed over the last several years that there seems to be a lack of a strong, positive Christian presence in our world. Despite what others may say, this waning Christian influence is not the fault of the media, government, education, entertainment, politics, or any other secular group. In my opinion, the fault lies squarely in the Christian community: many Christians simply do not act like Christians.

More and more Christians seem to be listening to Satan's lie that we must not talk about our faith in public—that expressing our faith is okay at home and in church, but our spiritual beliefs are a "personal matter." And it's no wonder Satan wants us to keep quiet outside of the church and home. For every preacher delivering sermons in a church, there are thousands of people in the marketplace who have opportunities to share the gospel in their daily interactions with others.

Jesus intends for us to integrate our faith with all aspects of our daily lives—including the marketplace. After all, as Ed Silvoso points out in his insightful book *Anointed for Business*, Christ was a businessman; He was a carpenter until He started His ministry at age thirty. Not only was Christ a businessman, but His disciples were also businessmen. They were fishermen, tax collectors, physicians, shepherds, and farmers—in short, they were all businessmen.

And interestingly, many of the miracles Jesus performed were not in the temple, but outside, in the marketplace. He did not limit His teaching to the formal services of the synagogue, either. Much of

Jesus's ministry occurred as He was going about His day in the marketplace, interacting with the people God had put in His path.[1]

Like Jesus and the disciples, we, too, must take our witness into the marketplace, on our jobs, and into all the corners of our everyday lives. That is exactly what an elderly lady from Tullahoma, Tennessee, did when I met her through a business associate in 1972.

A LITTLE LADY WITH A BIG FAITH

Sister Jessie was just a wisp of a lady, but her faith was mighty. I was so intrigued by her that I invited her to spend the Fourth of July weekend at my home. She walked in the front door talking about Jesus, and three days later she walked out of the front door talking about Jesus. *Jesus, Jesus, Jesus.* Every word was praise for her Lord and Savior, Jesus. She spoke of His love and mercy, of the great sacrifice He made on the cross to save us from sin and death.

She made a strong case for me to give my life to Him, and her words fell on the fertile soil of my heart. I went to bed thinking about what Sister Jessie said, and I woke up a new creature in Christ. There were no big fireworks—just a deep, abiding faith that I'd never be the same ol' Zig again. I had been made new, and like Sister Jessie, I wanted to tell people about Jesus.

TAKING JESUS TO THE MARKETPLACE

As a new believer, I was stunned when well-meaning friends and colleagues told me that I must not talk about my faith from the speakers' platform because it would ruin my career. The Holy Spirit, fortunately, moved in my heart and I felt strongly that it would be terribly wrong to heed their advice. From that day until this, I have not hidden my core identity: I am a witness for Jesus Christ. I have made my faith an integral part of my books and each of my presentations. Regardless of whom I'm speaking for, all I do is paraphrase the Bible, throw in some human-interest stories, and tell some funnies.

Did sharing my faith in Jesus Christ destroy my career? The answer is a resounding no! I'm extraordinarily grateful to say that for more than thirty-five years, I haven't solicited a single speaking engagement and I do not have a booking agent. The reason is very simple: God's Word does not return void, even if it's been paraphrased. People are seeking truth today more than ever before. They are hungry for spiritual knowledge and thirsty for that which will set them free—the person of Jesus Christ, my Lord and Savior.

The podium isn't the only place I speak about Jesus. He comes up in my conversations with individuals I'm seated next to on airplanes. I talk about Him in restaurants, in line at the cafeteria, in the grocery store, at the bank, in the dry cleaners. Every place I go is an appropriate place to talk about Jesus.

When I committed my life to Christ, every facet of my life was radically changed for the better. I became a new creature and quickly learned that God's possibles are infinitely greater than man's permissibles. As a born-again Christian, I wanted to make decisions that were consistent with my faith, and I became acutely aware of my responsibility to represent Him well. I asked God to remove temptation from my life so that I could focus on Him without distractions and to help me be about the business of telling others about Him and His love. He has honored that prayer, and I have been humbled by the number of people He has allowed me to share Him with, not only at church but also in the marketplace.

I can only imagine the revival that would take place if all Christians lived according to His Word and then took their love for Him into the marketplaces of their lives!

Christians who aren't afraid to be politically incorrect are helping change the hearts of people. This book is full of stories about men and women who are speaking up about God in places where doing so is generally considered unacceptable. More and more Christians are taking God into the corporate offices, board rooms, and break rooms where they work.

BIBLICAL PRINCIPLES AT WORK

In February 2003, I woke up with a thought so ironic I couldn't get back to sleep. The chances are high that few major corporations—particularly if they are publicly held corporations—permit Bible studies in the corporate offices. Many corporations forbid even talk of faith and in many cases, it's not exactly conducive to career building to have a Bible sitting on your desk, even if you read it only during your breaks.

The irony is simply this (and when God impressed this in my mind I almost laughed out loud): you can't have Bible study at the company where you work, but if you don't follow biblical principles while working there, your career will be very short-lived!

Here's what I'm getting at: To be a good employee you must obey the Ten Commandments. You've got to be a hard worker. You've got to be dependable, honest, sincere, committed to the company's well-being, give it your best shot at all times, be kind to your fellow employees, and just in general employ character qualities that are good—qualities that just happen to come directly out of the Bible! Embezzle from your company and you are toast, show up only two days a week and they give you your pink slip, kill somebody on the job and you can count on it, your career is over. So corporate America is saying, "We're not going to let you study the Bible, but if you don't obey it, you'll be fired!"

As I said, I got a huge charge out of that revelation. And it inspired me to write this book, so I could introduce you to men and women who have, like me, taken Jesus with them into the marketplace. They have spoken openly about Jesus, and their behavior toward others is noticeably and wonderfully different. Christians who live to be pleasing to God are so spiritually attractive that people want to know what makes them stand apart.

The men and women you will meet in this book are doing things God's way—and their lives demonstrate that God's way is still the best way! By integrating their faith with all areas of their lives, they have found joy and contentment in their careers, are experiencing Christ-centered family life, and have made huge contributions to society. I can personally testify that their biblical and spiritual approach to life has given them a peace that passes all understanding. I have learned from many of these people that doing things God's way leads to better business practices and that His greatest blessings are, as I like to say, the things that money can't buy!

You Will Know Them by Their Fruit

In His Sermon on the Mount, Jesus tells this parable: "You will know them by their fruits. Grapes are not gathered from thorn bushes nor figs from thistles, are they? So every good tree bears good fruit, but the bad tree bears bad fruit. A good tree cannot produce bad fruit, nor can a bad tree produce good fruit. Every tree that does not bear good fruit is cut down and thrown into the fire. So then, you will know them by their fruits" (Matthew 7:16–20).

Throughout the New Testament, the writers use the metaphor of "fruit" to describe the outward expression of the inward work of the Holy Spirit in believers' lives. Fruit is very simply the character of the Lord Jesus that flows out of transformed Christians. The fruit of the Holy Spirit can readily be seen in the lives of those who have received Him.

In Galatians 5:22–23, the apostle Paul outlines what the fruit of the Holy Spirit looks like in our daily lives: "The fruit of the Spirit is love, joy, peace, patience, kindness, goodness, faithfulness, gentleness, self-control." In this book, we will take an in-depth look at each of these nine characteristics as we observe how these men and women have effectively displayed the fruit of the Spirit in the marketplace. I hope you'll seek the intimate relationship they have with Christ and that you'll be inspired to emulate the godly lifestyles these men and women live.

In part 1, we will examine the fruit of the Holy Spirit that comes from within—love, joy, and peace. These stories clearly show how Christians can exemplify this inward fruit to glorify their King. When Christians are filled with the Holy Spirit, they are overwhelmed with love, joy, and peace. Their inward identity perceives with the heart of Christ and they recognize how their past behavior has broken the heart of God. The magnitude of the grief that follows drives believers to a depth of repentance they never knew was possible. The end result is a cleansing from sin and guilt that is a beautiful sight to behold.

In part 2, we'll consider men and women who display the outward fruit of the Holy Spirit—patience, kindness, and goodness. This fruit is the outward expression of the love, joy, and peace the Holy Spirit places within. People who know the abiding love of Christ experience joy even in the midst of grief and the peace that only a deep, intimate relationship with Jesus can produce. Love, joy, and peace manifest as patience, kindness, and goodness, all of which are easily identified as the outward fruits of a Christ-filled life. Outward fruits are simply the ones that can be seen by watching how someone interacts with others.

In part 3, we'll read about the fruits of a believer that are directed upward, toward Jesus—faithfulness, gentleness, and self-control. All of these, I believe, are more apparent as a believer matures in his or her relationship with Christ. The longer we are in relationship with Him, the more respectful we are of His holiness, the more gentle we are in our approach to our Beloved and others. The deeper our faith grows, the more steadfast we are in our faithfulness. And self-control is, for most Christians, a process, not an event. The longer we live and walk with Christ, the better we get at self-control.

Finally, in part 4, we'll read the firsthand account of my granddaughter's inspiring transformation from a life of sin and despair to one of joyously serving God. Then I will give you an opportunity to search your heart for the fruit that is in (or absent from) your own life. It is my prayer that if the fruit is absent, you will be inspired to find out why and do what it takes to turn your life over to Him. Ultimately, I will detail several simple, comfortable ways to start conversations about faith and belief in Jesus with anyone in the marketplace of your life.

The people you will meet throughout this book all have an inspiring love for Jesus Christ. They live their lives to be pleasing, obedient, and available to God. Their joy and His love are unmistakably present . . . and that, my friend, is what sets them apart. To God be the glory!

If you have been wondering how to let the light of Christ shine through you, you're reading the right book. If you question your Christianity, you're reading the right book. If you want to live effectively for Jesus Christ and you're not sure what that might entail, you are reading the right book.

Ultimately, the overwhelming and refreshing truth you will find in the pages that follow is that God's way is still the best way!

PART ONE

THE INWARD FRUIT *of the* SPIRIT

CHAPTER I

LOVE

We have come to know and have believed the love which
God has for us. God is love, and the one who abides in
love abides in God, and God abides in him.

—1 JOHN 4:16

As the above scripture describes, the gentlemen in the next two stories have been filled with God, Who is love. God clearly abides in Truett Cathy, and the evidence that He abided in John J. Eagan is indisputable.

Truett Cathy and John J. Eagan loved the people who have worked for them in ways that astound "normal" business leaders. Both men dared to care. You ask about their motive? Simply, the love of Christ overflowing into the lives of others.

I like to say that duty makes us do things well, but love makes us do things beautifully. Read on to see how business is done beautifully.

Truett Cathy

By this we know that we love the children of God, when
we love God and observe His commandments.

—1 John 5:2

One of my favorite people and examples of a follower of Christ who has taken his faith into the marketplace is Truett Cathy and the way he has managed his successful, nationwide restaurant chain, Chick-fil-A.

Truett was raised during the Depression years and is very humble, wise, and effective in what he does. His first restaurant, The Dwarf Grill, later renamed The Dwarf House, was where he initiated biblical principles into his management style. Truett took seriously God's command to rest on the Sabbath (Exodus 20:8–10), so he did not open on Sundays.

Sometimes doing things God's way involves a degree of risk. The Bible clearly states that risk taking is to be expected as we follow Christ and Christian principles. When Truett Cathy started opening Chick-fil-A stores in shopping malls, he was told that he would have to keep his stores open on Sunday. He adamantly refused, and because his company was so successful and highly respected in the business world, the shopping malls made an exception, permitting him to close his stores on Sundays.

The shopping malls were the only locations in which Chick-fil-A stores operated the first twenty years the chain was in business. Today, there are more than thirteen hundred restaurants in thirty-seven states and Washington, D.C., and you can buy delicious Chick-fil-A sandwiches from free-standing units, drive-through outlets, and even licensed outlets in hospitals, airports, business and industrial sites, and on college campuses. None of those locations is open on Sundays . . . and the Lord has blessed Truett Cathy's faithfulness. *Quick Service Restaurant* magazine named Chick-fil-A "Best Drive-Thru in America" four out of the past five years, and in 2006, Chick-fil-A's systemwide sales reached more than $2.275 billion—a 15.16 percent increase, extending Chick-fil-A's consecutive sales growth to thirty-nine remarkable years.

Chick-fil-A, being a private company, is able to do a variety of things with available resources. Chick-fil-A offers team members who work in the stores a one-thousand-dollar scholarship to the college of their choice based upon the recommendation of their operators. To date, they have awarded twenty thousand scholarships. Chick-fil-A also has a very low turnover of management personnel. One of the main benefits is the fact that employees can worship if they choose to and be with their families on Sundays.

Not only does Truett Cathy practice the biblical principle of resting on the Sabbath, but his life also evidences a sincere love for others, which is the fruit of the Spirit I want to highlight in this story. Truett has a love for children who for various reasons cannot live in their own homes. More than twenty-five years ago, he opened his home to them.

Because of his desire to help children, in 1984 Cathy established a charitable foundation called WinShape Centre Foundation. In addition to a college scholarship program and Camp WinShape®, the foundation also supports WinShape Homes®, which provides foster children with a stable, caring family environment. The following information from their Web page says it so well, I'm not even going to attempt to say it better!

WinShape Homes was created as a long-term foster care program for children who desperately need a caring family environment. S. Truett Cathy built this program to give children a chance to become all they can and desire to be.

Through the WinShape Homes program, a natural home environment is established, with two full-time, paid parents and up to 12 children in each foster home.

Currently, there are 12 WinShape Homes: eight in Georgia, two in Tennessee, and one each in Alabama and Brazil.

While many foster situations require children to leave to be on their own at 18, WinShape encourages and supports college attendance and a continued relationship with their parents and family. Children are encouraged by their foster parents and by WinShape to consider their foster home their true, permanent home, to return to on weekends and vacations.

WinShape Homes also benefits from the Chick-fil-A® Bowl, noted as the leading bowl in charitable giving. WinShape has received nearly $1 million since becoming a Chick-fil-A Bowl beneficiary in 1998.[1]

Truett Cathy invests his time, his money, and his love in helping orphans and foster children become all they can be. He also takes great pleasure in having his immediate family involved in his business. His wife has been a steady supporter and influence in his life and his sons work with him as well. Dan, his oldest son, is now president and COO of the company.

Truett Cathy follows biblical principles in every area of his life, and his son Dan does the same thing. I've had the privilege of speaking to their organization several times, and my wife and I regularly enjoy Chick-fil-A sandwiches and other goodies. We are consistently impressed with the courtesy and efficiency of the young men and women who work there. Their gratitude for their jobs is apparent. Chick-fil-A is an equal opportunity, biblically based company that contributes to all of society.

Anyone who has ever had the pleasure of meeting Truett Cathy knows he has a heart that is bigger than Texas. May we all desire and seek to be more and more like Jesus Christ, so that when people see us, they'll see the same kind of love that Truett Cathy has for Christ and for others.

JOHN J. EAGAN

In everything, therefore, treat people the same way you want them to treat you, for this is the Law and the Prophets.

—MATTHEW 7:12

John J. Eagan's American Cast Iron Pipe Company (ACIPCO) has entered into its second hundred years of existence and was named one of *Fortune* magazine's 100 Best Companies for eight consecutive years. The dream that began in the early 1900s was based on the decision of one man to honor his Lord and Savior and change the very bedrock upon which a successful manufacturing enterprise could be built.

John Eagan's vision to build a pipe manufacturing plant came about as a result of his God-given love for others, as demonstrated by his desire to provide sanitary conditions and clean drinking water to God's children who did not have them. A devout churchgoer and ardent practitioner of Scripture, John Eagan's original 1901 Bible sits in a glass case at the headquarters of ACIPCO in Birmingham, Alabama, opened to Matthew 7:12, the verse often called the Golden Rule: "In everything, therefore, treat people the same way you want them to treat you, for this is the Law and the Prophets."

John was respected and admired by his workers in an era when industrial capitalists usually looked upon organized labor with contempt. But unlike some of the more notorious capitalists of his day, Eagan was a Christian, and the Holy Spirit gave him a compassionate love for others that extended to his relationships with his workers. To Eagan, life and business were to be lived by the Golden Rule, and there would be no exceptions.

Despite the racial prejudice in America prior to World War I, Eagan chose to use management information from the greatest leadership book ever written to make a difference. To this end, he devoted the last years of his young but effective life to correcting the ills of an industry and implementing a business model that still serves subsequent generations with pride, dignity, and extraordinary effectiveness.

So what is unique about a manufacturing plant built on biblical principles? One difference is that the company puts the Golden Rule into action by including the voice of labor in management decisions. Sources at ACIPCO feel that, to the best of their knowledge, its form of representational leadership is still unlike any other company in the world. At ACIPCO, the board of operatives is elected by wage earners, and this elected group in turn advises the board of management and acts as a liaison between labor and management. These two groups form the board of trustees, who then elect the board of directors.

The background of the board is as unique as the system that elects them. People from the finance community, educational community, the customer pool, and one representing local social issues are part of the varied demographic of the board of directors. In addition, since the death of John Eagan's widow, one director position alternates between his son, Bill Eagan, and his daughter, Ann Goodhue. This means that the organization focused more on the employee and business families to run the enterprise than on any preconceived plan to have the family run the operation.

As early as 1912, ACIPCO provided bathhouses with hot and cold running water for all employees. Having determined that the health and dignity of workers was important for morale and eventual efficiency, Eagan instituted systems that would promote safety, sanitary conditions, and bonus programs that would let people share in the profits. Medical services for all employees and families were available as early as 1916, and sanitary toilets were installed in the foundry in the same time period. Again I would like to remind you that this was a time in America when racial prejudice was extremely high, and John Eagan's philosophy to live and conduct his life by the Word of God brought many of these radical changes to fruition.

John Eagan's prayer life was very much at the center of everything he did. He was known to pray diligently for God's will in the lives of all races of men, which was very progressive in his day and time. Though he considered himself unworthy, he asked the Lord to use him for His glory and to make him more mindful of others than he was of himself, a trait that was readily apparent to anyone who observed how he related to the people in his life. It was John Eagan's prayer that God would direct his steps and that he would always remember that everything he had belonged to God.

He committed himself to doing what he believed God would have him do in his business. Every humanitarian act that resulted in a better work environment for the employees of ACIPCO was the result of John Eagan doing what he felt his heavenly Father would have him do to glorify Him.

John submitted to the biblical requirement of tithing (giving 10 percent of one's income to the church) at a very tender age, and he committed 100 percent of his life as a living sacrifice as John became the man God intended him to be. As a Sunday school superintendent at the Presbyterian church in 1900, John insisted on publishing in the church bulletin the names of children from their Sunday school who were on their school's honor roll. This simplest form of recognition led many of his Sunday school students to prominent leadership roles later on in the life of that church.

John's love for others continued to be evident in his interest for underprivileged kids to get a decent education amid the degradation and poverty that existed in some of those areas. All this passion from someone who never finished high school, yet a wisdom that got him invited to Washington as a prominent industrialist who could help redesign the industrial landscape of the early 1900s.

After World War I ended, the young men of color who had patriotically served their country in embarkation camps and in the navy were returning to civilian life with little or no education. This, coupled with the reorganization of the Ku Klux Klan, made for a new crusade for John Eagan, who believed strongly that all men are created equal. Correspondence between John Eagan and the prison commission in Georgia to visit one of their camps shows his deep-rooted commitment to the conditions of all of humanity. Add to this his own strategic vision for ACIPCO, which included equal treatment for all of his employees, and you understand why Eagan did not want his employees to belong to any of the organized unions of his day; they did not allow people of color to be members. He chose not to fraternize with those who condoned racism or accepted it as a necessary evil to do business. He was determined to leave a legacy that included blessings and opportunities for all of God's children.

Unlike many religions that have graced this earth, Christianity offers the biblical principle of succession planning. The methodology behind succession planning is for everyone involved in the operation to understand vision and mission and then provide the directive for who will carry which task forward. Modeling his business precepts on how Christ chose His disciples to move His message and ministry to the world, John Eagan slowly but surely instituted the same philosophy in ACIPCO. All those who were part of the family were encouraged early and often to think of the legacy of goodwill and success they could leave behind. Just like Jesus called His disciples to be made "fishers of men" (Matthew 4:19; Mark 1:17), John paid bonuses to the employees of ACIPCO and gave them more than they could ever expect from a manufacturing plant in Alabama in the 1920s. The pride that resulted in the lives of those early workers quickly spread, and ACIPCO became the place where people wanted to work.

John Eagan passed away in March 1924; thus began a legacy that would thrive for the next seven and a half decades and beyond. Today, other companies have been acquired by ACIPCO and work under Eagan's philosophy of caring for the workers. Some of the individual practices may vary by type of industry and location, but the Golden Rule of business is practiced in all of these entities.[2]

John J. Eagan was obedient to God's Word by ensuring that his company operated on God's principles, and to this day employees of ACIPCO and its subsidiary organizations are reaping the benefits of Eagan's fruit of love.

CHAPTER 2

JOY

*These things I have spoken to you so that My joy may
be in you, and* that *your joy may be made full.*
—John 15:11

Brian Buffini and Jim and Naomi Rhode lead lives that demonstrate the inward fruit they have in common—joy! Joy, delight, gladness, and elation are emotions of the Holy Spirit.

These three people marvel at the joy in their lives and want others to have the same joy and fulfillment they have. As you read about their ministries and the way their work and faith comingle, consider how sharing Jesus can become a natural extension of what you already do. Help spread the joy!

Brian Buffini

Though you have not seen Him, you love Him, and though
you do not see Him now, but believe in Him, you greatly
rejoice with joy inexpressible and full of glory.

—1 Peter 1:8

Brian Buffini is the chairman and founder of Buffini & Company, America's largest one-on-one business coaching and training company. He and his wife, Beverly, are enjoying phenomenal success in each area of life. Their business is truly outstanding, their marriage is remarkable, and they are extremely close to their six children. They've done it all by following biblical principles in their personal, family, and business lives.

I read Brian's book, *Oh, By the Way . . .* , because I had been engaged to speak for them and I wanted to know as much as possible about their organization.[1] I was fascinated by the concepts he brought to light, as well as the spectacular results Buffini & Company was achieving, so I called and asked if my son and I could visit his company.

Our tour of their facilities was an amazing and delightful experience. I was introduced to almost three hundred people, all of whom were busily engaged in their work. I was blown away by the spirit of the organization—the employees' enthusiasm, the love they had for one another, their commitment to what they were doing, their effectiveness as they filled their roles in such a meaningful way. When I saw all that was happening, I knew I wanted our company to be part of what they were doing. I also knew that if we applied the principles they were teaching, we would benefit.

By now I'm sure you're wondering what sets Brian Buffini apart, so I'm going to tell you. Brian is an immigrant from Ireland. He grew up the son of a house painter in Dublin, where his father and grandfather taught him many important guiding principles that he practices to this day. Of all the principles he learned, one that stood out in his mind was when his granddad would visit the job site he was working on, look at his work, and ask, "Well, would you put your name to that?" If Brian truly couldn't put his name to the work he had done, his grandfather made him do it over.

Brian has instilled the level of integrity and the core values his grandfather taught him throughout Buffini & Company, where it is evidenced by his clients' loyal support. His grandfather's principles are proudly evident today in one of the company's three core values, "Excellence is our minimum standard!"

When Brian moved to America, he began selling real estate. After struggling with cold calls and the door-knocking methods he was taught, he finally applied his grandfather's principle of putting his name to what he did every day. This perspective literally jump-started his career, and he began making lots of sales. However, even though he was enjoying the increase in sales and a rapidly rising income, he was struggling with his personal life.

Brian had been in real estate about eighteen months when his success started becoming apparent to fellow church members. He was asked to teach a Sunday school class, so he developed a twelve-week course built on seven biblical principles of doing business. He taught it to a class of two hundred adults, and it took off like wildfire!

About eight weeks into teaching the class, Brian began to have difficulty sleeping at night. Slowly he became aware that there was some incongruence between how he was working every day as opposed to the principles he was teaching in Sunday school. He told his wife, "I need to stop teaching my class." Beverly replied, "Well, honey, why don't you just change your life and live the principles you've been teaching?" Leave it to a loving, understanding wife to get right to the root of his problem! Immediately, Brian began committing himself to plan his work every day according to the following seven separate and distinct principles.[2]

THE SEVEN BIBLICAL PRINCIPLES OF THE REFERRAL PROCESS

1. Why Does the Referral Process Work? When we work hard for the benefit of others, we will be rewarded.
"Do not be deceived, God is not mocked; for whatever a man sows, this he will also reap. For the one who sows to his own flesh will from the flesh reap corruption, but the one who sows to the Spirit from the Spirit will reap eternal life. Let us not lose heart in doing good, for in due time we reap if we do not grow weary. So, then, while we have opportunity, let us do good to all people." *Galatians 6:7–10*

2. How Are We to Serve Our Clients? By putting our clients and their needs ahead of our own.
"Do nothing from selfishness or empty conceit, but with humility of mind regard one another as more important than yourselves; do not merely look out for your own personal interests, but also for the interests of others." *Philippians 2:3–4*

3. How Are We to Plan? Plan to glorify and honor God in all that you do and trust Him to guide you in your work.
"Commit your works to the LORD and your plans will be established." "The mind of man plans his way but the LORD directs his steps." "Trust in the LORD with all your heart and do not lean on your own understanding. In all your ways acknowledge Him and He will make your paths straight." *Proverbs 16:3, 9; 3:5–6*

4. How Are We to Work? *We are to work as if God is our employer, and we are to treat each client the way we think God would want us to treat Him.*

"Whatever you do, do your work heartily as for the Lord rather than for men, knowing that from the Lord you will receive the reward of inheritance. It is the Lord Christ whom you serve." *Colossians 3:23–24*

5. How Are We to Use Our Gifts? *We are to use all the gifts God has given us to His glory.*

"The one who had received the five talents came up and brought five more talents, saying, 'Master, you entrusted five talents to me. See, I have gained five more talents.' His master said to him, 'Well done, good and faithful slave. You were faithful with a few things, I will put you in charge of many things; enter into the joy of your master.'" *Matthew 25:20–21*

6. To Fulfill Our Potential, We Must Constantly Commit to Grow. *Study daily the Word of God so that you can know for sure what God would have you do in all the circumstances of your life.*

"Therefore I urge you, brethren, by the mercies of God, to present your bodies a living and holy sacrifice, acceptable to God which is your spiritual service of worship. And do not be conformed to this world but be transformed by the renewing of your mind, so that you may prove what the will of God is, that which is good and acceptable and perfect." *Romans 12:1–2*

7. The Ultimate Goal of Our Work, Our Business, and Our Lives. *Live in such a way that people you serve will want to know what you have in your life that makes you so joyful, contented, and at peace.*

"Let your light shine before men in such a way that they may see your good works, and glorify your Father who is in heaven." *Matthew 5:16*

As soon as Brian began to apply the godly principles he had been teaching others, his real estate career took off like a rocket. Even though a great number of real estate agents do much of their business, including open houses, on Sundays, Brian made a commitment not to work on Sunday—to take that day off from a thriving business to honor the Lord and stay at home with his growing family. The Lord honored his faithfulness by doubling his income throughout every one of those five years. In 2004, Brian's business was up more than 1,200 percent over a banner 2003, and his profits were also up more than 1,200 percent. It really is true that God's way is still the best way!

After a period of time, Brian's success in real estate became more and more noticeable to the local market and to the real estate business at large. Ultimately, several companies, including well-known seminar speakers, invited him to speak about the easy-to-use systems he used in his business. It didn't take him long to discover that almost the entire real estate industry was doing their lead generation and sales in a manner directly opposite of his. They were cold-calling using the phone book. They were door knocking. They were sitting out on the weekends hosting open houses and eating cookies while they waited for a "hot prospect" to find them.

Brian's method, surprisingly, was much simpler. When he completed a business transaction following the seven biblical principles, he knew he had served his client in such a way that he had exceeded their high expectations. Consequently, he felt comfortable saying, "Oh, by the way, if you know of someone who is thinking about buying or selling a home and would appreciate the same kind of service I provided you, just give me their name and number and I'll be happy to follow up with them." And his clients did. They referred him, and referred him, and kept referring him because of the biblical principles he applied in doing business with them. He had served them better than they expected, and they referred him with confidence.

One of the biblical principles Brian's business is built on is found in the book of Philippians, where the apostle Paul says, "Do nothing from selfishness or empty conceit, but with humility of mind regard one another as more important than yourselves" (2:3). That means that he puts the needs of his clients before his own.

Invitations for Brian to be a motivational speaker increased. Every time he spoke, he unashamedly shared biblical principles, as well as the practical, how-to steps that went along with them. He enthusiastically taught his audiences from a variety of industries how they could also do business by referral and sort and qualify their database simply by following through and serving people in a manner beyond what was expected.

The more audiences Brian addressed, the more requests for speaking engagements came his way. Eventually, his wife, Beverly, who had heard him speak to audiences on many occasions, said, "Honey, you have a gift, and you need to give this gift back to the marketplace." Being a smart fellow, Brian listened to his wife and founded what is now called Buffini & Company, based on the core values learned from his grandfather, and the biblical principles in which he so strongly believes.

In only twelve short years, Brian and Beverly have grown the company into the largest one-on-one business coaching company in America, using three core principles:

1. Live what we teach.
2. Practice servant leadership.
3. Excellence is our minimum standard.

Brian has come to realize that the seminars he now conducts are similar to meetings an evangelist might hold. People get really excited about what he is teaching. However, Brian knows that after evangelism, there needs to be discipleship. So discipleship in his training system comes through one-on-one coaching.

Brian teaches his staff of more than three hundred well-trained people what servant leadership in the chain of command looks like by pointing them to the Bible. Jesus Himself held the greatest management seminar in history when he demonstrated to the apostles what servant leadership looked like. It was common in Jesus's day, when people wore sandals, for them to take off their shoes and wash their dirty feet before they would recline for dinner. The task of washing feet was considered too lowly a job for even a slave to perform for someone else. But Jesus, wanting to teach the disciples to serve others, washed the feet of all His disciples, and in doing so, illustrated the true meaning of servant leadership (John 13:3–11).

Brian implements this principle at Buffini & Company. The leadership of the company serves the interests of the employees ("washes their feet"), so that in turn, the employees willingly serve the customers. In business and in life, that's what servant leadership is all about.

Brian calls his seminars "Brian Buffini's Turning Point Retreat." From the outset, he never dreamed he'd be involved in this kind of growing, successful business. By applying biblical principles for the twelve consecutive years Buffini & Company has been in business, the company has averaged an 87 percent annual growth rate. They've been blessed beyond their wildest dreams, and they continue to grow through the daily referrals of satisfied clients. In addition, when he prepares to speak to an audience—which he does quite often—Brian, his wife, and his children all pray God's blessings and God's protection on each person in attendance. He has some fascinating stories about people who have commented to him what it means to them to know that he and his family were praying for them.

He says the turning point in his career came when he chose to implement biblical principles into his business, and to follow them no matter what the cost or financial burden. He made himself a promise that biblical principles would be the criteria for how he made his decisions and he learned that when your values are clear, your decisions are easy.

Brian Buffini says, "It's a good life! God has been very good to me, and He continues to be. I wish this kind of blessing for every-body, and I encourage, exhort, and challenge every Christian who says they believe in the Lord to put their beliefs into action."

Brian's single favorite quote is "Share the gospel at all times, but only use words if absolutely necessary." It is his passion as a Christian man to do exactly that. He wants people to recognize his commitment to Christ simply by watching his life. He invites others to get to know the God who blesses him and enjoys sharing the joy of the Lord with his brothers and sisters in Christ.

JIM AND NAOMI RHODE

I hope to come to you and speak face to face, so that your joy may be made full.

—2 JOHN 12

Jim and Naomi Rhode will tell you that God's way, in every way, is still the best way, and they have discovered that in each area of their lives. A unique couple with many similar interests, Jim and Naomi have been married fifty years and are the proud parents of three children who have blessed them with twelve grandchildren. One of the things that makes the Rhodes unique is that each of them has served a term as president of the National Speakers Association. Naomi also served as president of the International Federation for Professional Speakers in 2005–2006. During the year she held that office, she traveled around the world twice and spoke in nine different countries on its behalf.

Jim and Naomi received the Pioneer Award for their business, Smart Health/Smart Practice, which has divisions in dentistry and many of the healthcare professions. By following biblical principles in their lives and careers, they have discovered that they really can have it all by doing things God's way.

The Rhodes' business employs five hundred people in Phoenix, Arizona; more than five thousand people worldwide; and has reached a volume of more than $100 billion a year. Their employees know the company is based on strong Christian values, and they can expect to be treated well as a result of that foundation. All of the above undoubtedly contributed to Jim being named entrepreneur of the year for the state of Arizona.

Naomi shared with me that she is convinced that "as Christians we cloister ourselves in the comfort of the church rather than focusing on 'lifting high the cross in the marketplace'!" She certainly agrees that the church is the place to worship the Lord, to get built up in the Word, to grow spiritually, and to experience the joy of fellowship with other believers. But she stressed that one of the core beliefs she and Jim share is that "the church is meant to be a regular, refreshing oasis and not a camping ground." They have an ongoing awareness that being a Christian is not just a belief system, but a radical life transformation, stating, "Living our faith is always more impressive than speaking our faith."

Over the years I've encountered Jim and Naomi at National Speakers Association meetings, at worship services, at various seminars, and even in airports where we cross paths periodically. It's a delight to watch them in action. Naomi holds dear Matthew 5:14–16, which admonishes us, "You are the light of the world. A city set on a hill cannot be hidden; . . . Let your light shine before men in such a way that they may see your good works, and glorify your Father who is in heaven."

Jim has primary responsibility for running the business, but Naomi is very actively involved. When the Rhodes are invited to speak on Sunday, they offer to host an interdenominational Christian worship service for program participants who would ordinarily want to leave campus to find a place to worship. They recommend a meeting room with a thirty- to sixty-minute slot before the main meeting begins, and they lead the worship service by sharing a scripture and a devotional. They encourage the hosts to provide special music to enhance the services and to arrange for one or more of their attendees to share their own faith. And because much of their work is done in health care, Jim and Naomi often ask a dentist or physician to share a mission-trip experience as a challenge to get more of the attendees inspired to go outside their comfort zone and share their faith. They have had as many as eight hundred people attend these services.

As an additional part of their ministry, the Rhodes regularly buy cases of Bibles that can be read through in a year by reading just fifteen minutes a day. These Bibles are structured with daily readings from the Old Testament, New Testament, Psalms, and Proverbs. Naomi points out that in many of her speeches she challenges the audiences to read and often asks them to name the best books they've read. Almost always the Bible is mentioned. In her question-and-answer sessions, she usually mentions that the Bible is the best book she's ever read. She shares that she and Jim read the Bible out loud, cover to cover, in fifteen minutes a day, explaining how it works, and offers anyone who will commit to do it a free Bible in an easy-to-read translation, such as the New Living Translation.

Naomi says, "I use quotes and examples from Scripture in my speaking with sensitivity—depending on how long the speech is. It is always possible to work in a proverb, psalm, or example from Scripture. This engenders many comments and questions later from the audience, in line, over meals, and in correspondence."

Jim's favorite verse for business and speaking is Proverbs 24:3–4: "Any enterprise is built by wise planning, common sense, and profits wonderfully by keeping abreast of the facts" (TLB). He regularly shares this verse with audiences as a preface to his remarks.

Naomi points out that in more than thirty years of speaking almost every week, she has never been criticized for sharing the Scriptures. So much for Satan's admonition that our faith is a private matter—okay at home and in church, but not in the marketplace!

One of Jim and Naomi's favorite verses is Psalm 19:14: "Let the words of my mouth and the meditation of my heart be acceptable in Your sight, O LORD, my rock and my Redeemer." They ask God to show them who they are to share each meal with. Many participants have come to know the Lord as guests at one of those meals, which Jim and Naomi see as a special privilege that gives both of them great joy indeed.

Naomi shares a classic story to illustrate her habit of praying for those who will approach her after she speaks. After a morning speech in Williamsburg, a woman approached her and asked, "You are a Christian, aren't you?" She responded, "Yes, are you?" "No," the answer came quickly. Naomi then asked her, "Are you going to be?" The woman teared up and said, "Yes." Naomi asked, "When? Now would be a really good time, because none of us knows how much time we have." The woman agreed, and Naomi took her outside the meeting room, prayed with her, gave her a Bible she had in her briefcase, and then asked her (as she always does) if she knew anyone else in her life who loved Jesus. The lady responded, "Oh, yes, my husband does! I have been going with him to church for twenty years, sitting in the back row, not ready to believe. Today is my day!"

Being president of the four-thousand-member National Speakers Association in 1994 was an incredible honor to Naomi Rhode. She chose for her theme "The Privilege of the Platform," and in speaking for every state chapter, planning programming for the entire year, and writing more than two thousand personal letters, she had countless privileges to share her joy and God's glory through her life, love, lessons of leadership, and literal sharing of the glorious, good news of the gospel.

In a very loving and practical way, Jim and Naomi Rhode have taken advantage of the privilege of leadership, allowing them to influence the NSA selection committee chairpersons, programming, and theme. Referring to Jesus's encouragement for His followers to be "the salt of the earth" and "the light of the world" (Matthew 5:13–15), Naomi says, "Hopefully the salt shaker was busy that year, and the light was bright." Obviously, as president of the International Federation of Professional Speakers, Naomi continued to have significant opportunities to influence others for Christ's kingdom.

Jim and Naomi Rhodes' lives demonstrate clearly that God's way is truly the best way—at home, on the job, and in the community.

CHAPTER 3

PEACE

Peace I leave with you; my peace I give you. I do not give to you as the world gives. Do not let your hearts be troubled and do not be afraid.

—JOHN 14:27 NIV

Peace is that sense of wholeness, contentment, and stillness that fills a true believer. And it is possibly one of the most observable fruits to nonbelievers because it is something that is so obviously missing from their lives.

I can honestly say that I never lose sleep because of situations that are going on in my life. I am able to trust in God's plan, and I believe that His purpose is being achieved through the trials that come my way as well as through the successes.

Dr. Dick Furman, businessman Wayne Alderson, and Dr. Leslie Holmes are men who experience that kind of peace, the peace that passes understanding. Dr. Furman made a wise decision early on in his internship that replaced incredible stress with divine peace. Wayne Alderson took a volatile work atmosphere, infused it with the love of Christ, and saw peace prevail where anger had flourished. Dr. Leslie Holmes brought men with years of bitter opposition who knew no peace together in a safe place. All three men love and live for the Lord, as you'll see when you read their stories.

DR. DICK FURMAN

*In his heart a man plans his course, but the LORD deter-
mines his steps.*

—PROVERBS 16:9 NIV

Dick Furman, a physician from Boone, North Carolina, was one
of fifteen interns just beginning surgical training. The interns
knew that in one short year, only seven of them would be accepted
to become residents in the University of Kentucky surgical training
program. Competition was intense, and all fifteen interns were very
highly qualified. All of them worked hard, wanting to move on to
the residency program. They were on call every other night, requiring staying overnight at the hospital. On off nights they usually didn't
get home until 10 p.m. So much was expected of them, there was
little time left for anything else.

After three months of working as hard as he could, Dick Furman
realized there was no significant difference among the fifteen interns.
He considered what he could do to ensure himself a spot in the residency program, and the only area he found where he could make
an improvement was in the 8 a.m. surgical cases. All interns were
expected to meet on the floor at six thirty each morning and make
rounds with the residents on all of the patients on the team's service.
The residents and interns went from patient to patient together, seeing who would need discharging, who needed an IV restarted, who
needed dressings changed, and so on.

At the completion of rounds, the interns would go take care of
the patients' needs for the morning. The expectation was for the
interns to finish their work and be in the operating room by seven

thirty to perform a ten-minute scrub on their hands and forearms, followed by gowning and prepping the patient, and scrubbing the operative site for ten minutes. Next they placed sterile drapes on the patient, and at eight o'clock sharp the attending surgeon was to walk into the room ready to operate. The problem was, the interns were never there at seven thirty because they were still upstairs on the floor, starting IVs, writing discharge orders, or changing dressings on their patients. Result: interns rarely made it to the operating room on time, and the attending surgeon would arrive at eight o'clock to find he had to prep his own patient for surgery—and he was upset about that because the operating room crew had worked so hard to get the patient there on time in preparation for the operation.

Dick said one morning it came to him: he could be the only intern out of the fifteen to be on time to the operating room every morning. He knew what was expected of the interns, what time they were expected to be on the floor for rounds with the residents. But he decided to do more than was expected of him.

Dick began making rounds by himself, arriving to see his patients thirty minutes before the other interns arrived to start their day with their resident. No one told him to do it; he just set the goal to get up thirty minutes earlier and make his rounds on his own patients at 6 a.m. If his patients needed their IVs restarted, he would do it right then. If discharge orders needed to be written, he would write them; if dressings needed changing, he would change them. Then when the resident made rounds with him at six thirty, Dick's patients all looked great. Their IVs were going, the wounds had neat bandages, and sutures that needed to be removed were already removed.

After rounds, Dick helped the resident with his chores and occasionally even had time to eat breakfast with his resident. But one thing for certain: he was always in the operating room at seven thirty, and his patients were always prepped and ready to be operated on when the attending surgeon arrived promptly at eight o'clock.

None of the other interns followed his lead. When he decided to do more than expected, his life changed as an intern, as a resident, and eventually as a surgeon in practice.

As a direct result of this simple principle—*do more than expected*—Dick Furman was advanced to the status of resident's physician early. When one of the residents suddenly had to leave the program, the attending staff met to decide who should take his spot. Their decision was unanimous: they voted to promote Dick Furman to resident after only seven months of internship. Dick asked, "Was I given the privilege to do this because I was almost a half-year of training better than the others, or capable of performing advanced surgery which they were not capable of doing?" No, he had gotten the nod to move up the ladder early because of one simple principle: he had made a habit of doing more than expected. He stood out because he was the only intern who always had his patients ready for surgery at eight o'clock sharp. He says, "All I had to do was implement one simple principle: do more than expected!"

Dr. Furman has followed the principle of setting realistic goals all of his life. Dick, like all of us, had his own share of mistakes and setbacks. One of his investment opportunities required several years to bring the account back into balance. He strongly believes not only that failure is an event and not a person, but that he who has never failed cannot succeed. Failure has been his stimulus for success. He points out how the apostle Peter's greatest failure—denying Christ three times—was followed by his greatest success when after the resurrection Peter preached with such force and power that three thousand people came to know Christ as Lord and Savior.

As a surgeon, colleague, husband, father, and man of God, Dr. Furman clearly believes he should do everything "as to the Lord" (Ephesians 6:7). One of his favorite verses is Proverbs 16:9: "In his heart a man plans his course, but the LORD determines his steps" (NIV). With this in mind, each January Dick would write down the goals he wanted to accomplish as a surgeon for the year. His motto has always been, "Do all you're supposed to do—and then some. Do more than expected."

But Dick is also an entrepreneur at heart. One January, he set a goal to build a restaurant in his hometown, but he could not find the right restaurant to build. Two years passed before a friend told Dick about a new restaurant chain: Wendy's Old Fashioned Hamburgers. Dick drove five hours to the nearest Wendy's in Atlanta, Georgia. He liked the food, the service, and the concept, so he applied for a franchise. Initially, the company turned him down because they were not allowing stores to be built in small towns. Dick says he would never have looked at Wendy's had he not set that original goal of getting involved in the restaurant business. But he hung on to his dream, and six months later the partnership he, his friend, and his brother had formed was given the go-ahead to build three Wendy's in small towns in North Carolina.

Dick believes in the effectiveness of writing down your goals. Until he had written down and discussed a goal to own thirty-seven Wendy's restaurants with his partner, the original plan had been to add one or two new locations per year. He flew by the new goal when his partnership acquired a company in South Carolina that owned thirty franchises. Presently, they have seventy-six restaurants.

Dick Furman fervently believes that integrating your Christian values with your business success is critical. He believes real success—not *success* as many in our culture would define it, but a real success that satisfies—comes only when you look to the Lord to direct your steps and let Him use you in His service.

As Dick matured in his relationship with the Lord, he learned that the very best, most peaceful place for him to be was in the center of God's will for his life. He stopped setting self-serving goals and began to pray about each goal, asking God to close the door on any goal he set that did not fit into God's plan for his life.

Dick uses his talents as well as his financial success as a witnessing tool for his Lord. He and his oldest brother teamed up with Franklin Graham to found World Medical Mission, the medical arm of Samaritan's Purse. They encourage physicians to give four to six weeks a year out of their practice to travel overseas at their own expense to work in mission hospitals. In the first year, 1978, they sent only four doctors. Today, more than 250 physicians a year travel to those small mission hospitals around the world. World Medical Mission uses only physicians who are Christians and who follow Christian principles, because these doctors are replacing doctors who have given their full time of medicine to the mission field.

Dick Furman is a classic example of what a sold-out Christian can do by following biblical principles. In addition to being a successful surgeon, husband, father, and businessman, he has been honored by being elected president of the North Carolina chapter of the American College of Surgeons, president of the North Carolina Surgical Association, governor of the State of North Carolina for the American College of Surgeons, and a presenter at the national meeting of the American College of Surgeons for work overseas with Samaritan's Purse, World Medical Mission.

In keeping with his belief that the workplace is our witness and that how we do our job says worlds about our relationship with Christ, Dick's partnership, Tar Heel Capital, gives every one of their Wendy's employees a New Testament and each of their managers a Bible. Attached to the page inside the front cover is the following letter:

> Tar Heel Capital welcomes you to your new position with Wendy's. We are committed to helping you live a very successful life and having a prosperous future.
>
> The theme of our organization is "Serving Quality Food in a Christian Atmosphere." This has proven to be a key factor in our success, both in dealing with our employees and operating our restaurants.

Servanthood, as modeled by Christ, is a central principle of the Bible and of Tar Heel Capital. Therefore, we expect each employee to take a servant's attitude when dealing with our guests that dine at Wendy's. As we demonstrate a servant's attitude, each customer will know that he or she is the most important individual in our restaurant.

Another important Christian principle is the golden rule—"Do unto others as you would have them do unto you." Tar Heel Capital is committed to that standard in forming our relationship with you, our valued employee. We are interested in your personal development as well as your success in your employment.

By applying these principles and striving to give the most outstanding service possible to our guests, we are developing our stores into one of the best Wendy's franchises in the national system. This can be accomplished only with the help of you, as one of our dedicated employees.

I am presenting this Bible to you in hopes that you will allow its teaching to guide you in everything you do.[1]

Dick Furman's spiritual beliefs have influenced every area of his life . . . for the better!

When we, like Dr. Furman, fully understand that true peace and true success in life come only to those who put their trust and faith in Jesus Christ, then and only then will we look to the Lord to direct our steps and allow Him to use us for His purposes.

WAYNE ALDERSON

Be anxious for nothing, but in everything by prayer and supplication with thanksgiving let your requests be made known to God. And the peace of God, which surpasses all comprehension, will guard your hearts and your minds in Christ Jesus.

—PHILIPPIANS 4:6–7

Wayne Alderson can tell you that there are no hopeless situations—only people who lose hope in the face of some situations. Peace escaped the people who worked with Wayne at Pittron Steel. They felt hopeless because the future of Pittron Steel looked dubious at best, but Alderson decided to look beyond the obvious, and the rest is history.

In 1965, Wayne Alderson went to work for Pittron Steel, a steel foundry in Glassport, Pennsylvania. Initially, he was in the financial department. In four short years, he was promoted to controller and chief financial officer. That may all sound well and good, except the position of controller made Alderson responsible for the financial position of the company, which was bleak.

In the late 1960s and early '70s, steel mills weren't the nicest, cleanest places to work. The hot, sweaty, filthy environment seemed natural under the circumstances, but it created unrest and job dissatisfaction among the employees.

Tension was building between management and laborers when, in 1972, the United Steel Workers Union decided to strike. The decision wasn't an easy one to make. Steel mills had been shutting down all around them due to the same kind of financial problems Pittron was suffering, and the workers knew the strike might force Pittron to close its doors forever. But they had had enough. Many concessions had already been made by the union, and conditions were not improving. Extreme measures were needed to force change.

Just before the eighty-four-day strike, Wayne Alderson was promoted to vice president of operations. His management style proved to be the exact opposite of what had been in place before he accepted his new position. He called his plan to save Pittron "Operation Turnaround," and instead of the confrontational, in-your-face style of intimidation management previously used, Alderson's more peaceful approach sought the respect, and thus the cooperation, of his employees.

In an unprecedented move, Alderson agreed to meet in secret with then USWA Local 1306 president Sam Piccolo. He unveiled his plan for Operation Turnaround, and that meeting broke the tradition of gridlock between union and management. The relationship forged between the two men exists even to this day.

The steps Alderson took were the beginnings of his extremely well-received "Value of the Person—Theory R" management process that he presently teaches in seminars across the country.[2]

Alderson's example shows us that demonstrating love, dignity, and respect for employees can remove the circumstances that create mistrust, resentment, and thus anger and unrest in the workplace and instill security and peace instead. Both of these create a foundation for high performance. Alderson wanted to give back the dignity the men of Pittron deserved, and he began by making himself accessible to them. He went out of the clean corporate offices into the dirty foundry to meet the men on their turf.

Over a period of time, the promises Alderson made to Sam Piccolo came to fruition. Though he wasn't trusted initially and many of the men thought he was too good to be true, as time went along they learned that Wayne Alderson was the real thing. Men who had hated coming to work arrived with a happy countenance. They no longer felt like second-class citizens because they were no longer talked down to or treated shabbily by their bosses.

Racial prejudice was alleviated as men of all races were able to move into positions other than the only one that had previously been available to them, the position of "chipper." Known as the dirtiest and most undesirable position in the mill, being a chipper required the use of a hammer to remove defects from large steel castings. When Wayne Alderson asked one of the chippers to let him take a crack at it, he lasted only a few minutes at the difficult task. As he climbed down from the casting, he commented that whatever the company paid the man, he earned every cent of it. As Peter Grazier states in his article, "The Miracle of Pittron Steel," "By his gesture, Alderson had dignified the least respected task in the plant."[3] Valuing people was the key that turned Pittron Steel around.

Wayne Alderson is a man after God's own heart. When it was jokingly suggested that he start teaching his employees about the Bible, he began with informal discussions that eventually became Bible studies in a storage room directly under the open hearth furnace in the foundry. The men who attended encouraged others to attend, and what was originally thought to be a gimmick by some became the influence that changed their attitudes and their lives. Alderson's Bible study came to be known as the Chapel Under the Open Hearth. Visitors who heard about it and Operation Turnaround were amazed by the changes taking place. The workers were happy, and the number of grievances filed fell from about seven hundred a year to one per year. More than one thousand of the twelve hundred employees attended the Chapel Under the Open Hearth . . . all on their own time without pay.

Alderson understood that the workers needed to prosper because he lives his life to be pleasing to God. God holds His people responsible for creating an atmosphere in which He is recognized as the

Author of all things. At Pittron, Alderson set about changing the atmosphere by cleaning up the filth that surrounded the workers. He cleaned up the mill—painting, remodeling, and installing showers so the workers could wash up after their shifts and arrive home feeling refreshed and ready to spend time with their families. He created an atmosphere where employees could reach out, grow, and know that God was in control. A sense of peace had replaced the taunting and turmoil that prevailed when Alderson took over as vice president of operations.

In turn, the workers came to love and respect "Brother Alderson," as he was fondly called. One man told his wife that God was in the plant, that He had sent them a man who was serving God. Another commented that having Alderson in charge was like walking out into the sunlight after you've been in a dark room. Wives wrote letters of thanks to the foundry, saying their husbands were not as angry when they arrived home and that they were happier and spending more time together as a family.

The byproduct of positive change in the attitudes of the workers immediately showed in the corporate numbers. The best salespeople turned out to be the happy workers themselves, and sales increased 400 percent, taking the company from a $6 million deficit to a $6 million profit. The workforce quadrupled, absenteeism dropped to less than 1 percent, productivity rose by 64 percent, and total quality excellence was introduced into the marketplace.

These impressive numbers didn't go unnoticed. On October 23, 1974, the foundry was sold. A ripple of fear coursed through the workers as they heard the news and began to wonder if their leader and mentor would be asked to leave. Alderson reminded them that they were never to put their faith in a man, but in God, whom they could trust to see them through.

Amazingly, Wayne Alderson's radical management style of valuing people was not appreciated and he was ultimately terminated.

For the first time in twenty years, a new labor contract was reached without a strike, but the Value of the Person—Theory R foundation Alderson had put in place was severely tested by the new management. Twenty-one months later, the foundry was shut down by a wildcat strike.

What happened at Pittron Steel was nothing less than a miracle. Alderson said he thought it was very important that Christ had chosen to work this miracle in a foundry, because a coal mine was the dirtiest place to work. He points out that if God could save a filthy foundry that was ready to close its doors, then He could make a miracle just like the Pittron miracle happen anywhere, anywhere at all. All that had to happen was for management to value the workers.

To this day Wayne Alderson teaches others how to implement "Value of the Person—Theory R Leadership." When he politely refused to stop attending and teaching the Bible study in the Chapel Under the Open Hearth as he was asked to do by the new owners of Pittron Steel, Alderson knew his fate was being sealed. But he did not waver and he did not fear. The inward spirit of peace prevailed. He served a bigger Boss, and his calling was greater than the task at hand.

If all Christians in management positions across our great country lived and taught biblical principles the way Wayne Alderson does, *awesome* would be too insignificant a word to describe the transformation we would see in the workplace.

How can we implement Alderson's model of Christ-centered marketplace ministry in the generations to come? Fear not! Remember that we serve an awesome God. No problem is too big for Him! God will help those of us who are dedicated to seeking His will, obedient to His will, and living out His love in our homes, schools, churches, or the marketplace.

Dr. Leslie Holmes

If possible, so far as it depends on you, be at peace with all men.

—Romans 12:18

As a pastor in a denomination that has experienced considerable division over the years, Dr. Holmes has had plenty of experience using his people skills and biblical principles to bring opposing sides together. Over the years, Dr. Holmes has observed that among some evangelicals there is a tendency to denote certain "sins of the month," such as divorce, drinking, gambling, and abortion. In his denomination, each of these was presented as an offense worse than its predecessor, became a hot issue for a while, and was thoroughly beaten into the ground but never really defeated. The situation we're going to examine through Dr. Holmes's story involves not the sin of the month, but a sin of years and years and generations and generations—a sin that has destroyed peace in all its forms in Ireland.

Dr. Holmes believes that Christ wants us to do the best for all folks (regardless of what their sins are because all of us are sinners) and says, "Ministering will not come from persuading them to be like us, for we, too, are sinners, and that would be trading our sins for their sins, so they're no better off. Successful ministry, regardless of the sin, means helping sinners to become more like Jesus, and all of us need help in that area."

Leslie Holmes arrived in America in October 1967 at the age of twenty-two with a wife and a ten-month-old son. Their decision to come to the United States, a place they had only seen in the movies and in magazines, was based on their assumption that it would be a better place to raise their son than their hometown of Belfast, Northern Ireland.

Though his original plan was to move to America and make a million dollars, God had a better idea. About three months after he arrived, Leslie Holmes heard the gospel presented in a way that he had not heard in twenty-two years of attending church in Ireland. As a result, he committed his life to Christ. Within a few days, he realized that he wanted to spend the rest of his life telling others about the wonderful certainty of knowing eternal life through Jesus Christ.

It took five long years for him to find a way to begin his college education, but he didn't let that deter him. He was so anxious to preach that he pastored a tiny Presbyterian church in rural Mississippi while he finished college and seminary training in just five years and was awarded a fellowship to complete his doctoral studies.

Dr. Holmes's position in the church and his Irish heritage has put him in a unique position. Dr. Holmes said that after the Northern Ireland Good Friday Agreement was signed in 1998, many of the local media sought his opinion. From telephone conversations with government and clergy leaders earlier that week, he knew that getting this agreement passed was as near a miracle as anything he could imagine in Northern Ireland politics, so he immediately offered his church as a place where people of all political persuasions might gather to pray and thank God for what had happened. He knew that God's Word, prayer, and patience works wonders.

However, Dr. Holmes had difficulty persuading some local Roman Catholic leaders to join in leading the event, so he called two of his good Roman Catholic friends, Tom O'Donoghue, owner of the Blarney Stone Restaurant, and Dan Rooney, owner of the Pittsburgh Steelers, and asked for their assistance. Amazingly, the power of friendship was really effective because within an hour Dr. Holmes had full cooperation from the local Catholic Diocese and the public

relations team for one of the nation's leading football teams working with him. A few days later they hosted a crowd of nearly five
hundred people at a service in their church. Up front were clergy and
lay leaders representing all sides of the debate.

Just before the service began, Dr. Holmes heard there was a
group of protestors gathering outside the church. As he looked out
the window he saw about twenty people with a large banner, hand-
ing out leaflets. He could tell from the banner that their agenda was
politically motivated. Immediately he gathered six good-sized men
and walked out front to where these people were gathered. Their
signage revealed that they were representatives of one of the extreme
Protestant positions. "I asked them to move, and they refused at
first. Then after further conversation they agreed to go quietly and
did so," said Dr. Holmes.

He said what he didn't realize was that some media people who
were already set up for the services in the sanctuary followed them
out of the church and filmed what he said to the protesters. He said
God gave him both the courage and the words when he turned to
the media folks and said, "Tonight you can focus on the bad news
of this protest or on the good news of what is about to happen inside
the church. I hope you will choose well." To their credit, not one
media outlet made any mention of the protest; the next day the
media all prioritized what happened inside at the service for prayer
and peace. Many of them even quoted from his sermon.

A few days later, Dr. Holmes received a telephone call from
someone claiming to represent the extreme Catholic position. He
asked to meet with Dr. Holmes. Knowing that some members of the
extremist party are noted for violence, Dr. Holmes agreed to meet at
a neutral public setting. They met in the lobby of a well-known
downtown hotel, and for three hours the extremist told Dr. Holmes
at great length about his experience growing up as a Roman
Catholic in Ireland. Dr. Holmes listened, and as the meeting came to

a close the extremist said, "You know those protestors you asked to leave the front of the church? They were our fellows." That surprised Dr. Holmes because their banner and handouts all bore colors he knew to be associated with the Protestant side. The extremist confessed, "It was a kind of undercover operation." Then he went on to report how the night after the services he had entered a local Irish bar and that a group of his people were laughing about the fact that "they had looked so much like the opposition, the local Presbyterian minister was fooled. But," he added, "I pointed out that you had asked them to leave, even though it would be more natural for you to support that side. I told them I could work with you, and that's why I'm here."

What a marvelous approach Dr. Holmes took! Then the extremist went on to offer to have leaders from his side meet in Pittsburgh as long as leaders from the opposing side would meet. He also said, "I know they can never do that publicly for political reasons, but we have contacts who will pick people up from any airport in Europe on private jets and fly them to Pittsburgh without anybody knowing. There will be no cameras or recording equipment present, and we can get them into the U.S. without getting a stamp on their passports. Nobody will ever know that they were here."

Dr. Holmes said, "At his request, I made contact through a clergy friend in Northern Ireland. He in turn contacted some Northern Ireland government leaders. Soon a meeting was arranged, and one of the conclusions was that I would moderate the meeting at a neutral place in Pittsburgh."

Some days later they met, and at that meeting were a number of dignitaries with Irish interests and connections. They included Washington political personalities and well-known Pittsburgh business leaders, along with representatives from various political parties in Northern Ireland and the Republic of Ireland. Dr. Holmes opened the meeting by welcoming them and explaining the context of why they were together. "In the interests of being open, I told them I had been invited to have lunch with the First Minister of Northern Ireland next week, when I was scheduled to be in Belfast." Almost from the beginning, Dr. Holmes said, "The meeting got off to an acrimonious start. One side accused the other and the other responded in kind. After a couple of hours, we adjourned with no apparent change of position by anyone." He pointed out that it was truly a frustrating experience, as each went his separate way.

Then the unexpected happened. "Two days later, the extremist whom I had met in the hotel called me and said, 'Well, Reverend, that was a good meeting the other day.' Frankly," Dr. Holmes said, "I was stunned. I replied, 'I'm glad you enjoyed it. I sort of thought I'd heard all those same arguments for over thirty years.' He responded, 'Oh, I know. But it needed to be said again and I have some concessions from our people that we'd like to have you take to the First Minister when you meet with him in a few days. Would you be willing to do that?'" Dr. Holmes agreed. He delivered three important concessions as instructed and was asked to carry three more back to the extremist leader.

As the old saying goes, there are always three sides to an issue— your side, the other side, and the right side. When people begin to talk and listen, they start to understand each other. And then they become people and not "the other side," or even "the enemy."

Dr. Holmes said this experience shows what coming together to pray can do. Through that meeting at First Presbyterian Church of Pittsburgh, some small steps were made to advance peace in a part of the world where people have been fighting one another for generations. Perhaps even more important, he said, it helped demonstrate that in Christ these longstanding, deeply held positions can begin to come together, and the opposite of terrorism is not necessarily peace, but peace borne out of righteousness.

Yes, peace borne out of righteousness is what fills Dr. Holmes's life and spills over into the lives of those with whom he comes in contact. Today Dr. Holmes is pastor of Saxe Gotha Presbyterian Church in Lexington, South Carolina, where he is helping others by loving them like Jesus.

PART TWO

THE OUTWARD FRUIT *of the* SPIRIT

CHAPTER 4

PATIENCE

We desire that each one of you show the same diligence
so as to realize the full assurance of hope until the end,
so that you will not be sluggish, but imitators of those
who through faith and patience inherit the promises.

—HEBREWS 6:11–12

O ne of the marks of an authentic Christian is abiding patience and great endurance. This fruit of the Spirit comes with humility and trust in God.

Patience is a fruit of the Holy Spirit that is too often overlooked. People speak readily of the kindness, the love, and the joy in their lives or that they see in the lives of others. But these days we're all so busy, life is a whirlwind of activity, and we're moving so fast nobody stops long enough to even notice patience in others.

The consistent patience John McKissick showers on his football players by getting to know them and their parents, the patience Dr. Tony Evans displays toward his family and his congregation's growing ministries, and the patience and the time Jim Dawson invested to get to know his employees all had its foundation in this fruit of the Holy Spirit.

JOHN MCKISSICK

Consider it all joy, my brethren, when you encounter various trials, knowing that the testing of your faith produces endurance. And let endurance have its perfect result, so that you may be perfect and complete, lacking in nothing.

—JAMES 1:2–4

John McKissick's story is truly one of the most remarkable in the long history of football at any level, but it's more than just the story of a football coach. It's the story of a patient man who loves his God, his family, his community, and the players he coaches.

The year 2006 marked Coach John McKissick's fifty-fifth season coaching the Summerville High School football team near Charleston, South Carolina, and he finished it with a typical McKissick record, 12–1, the only loss occurring in the semifinal playoffs. He loves coaching and has no intention of quitting the job that he got because he was the only applicant who didn't ask how much it paid. According to a September 11, 2003, article by Jill Lieber in *USA Today* titled "Football Coach All Alone at Brink of 500 Wins," when he started, he was coaching the boys' and girls' basketball, baseball, and track teams. He taught five history classes, mowed and lined the football field, shined the football cleats, washed the game uniforms, and taped the players' ankles—all for $3,000 a year.[1]

In my conversations with him it is abundantly clear that although he has now celebrated his eightieth birthday, John's zest and passion for what he does are that of a much younger man. With a 12–1 record, I doubt many people would claim he has diminished in effectiveness. His record of 543–128–13 in fifty-five seasons speaks for itself.

Let's dig a little deeper and take a closer look at this remarkable man. When twenty-five-year-old Coach McKissick started coaching and teaching at Summerville High School, it was one of the smallest schools in South Carolina and Harry Truman was president. Eleven presidential terms later, John McKissick, without making another move, finds himself coaching at one of the largest schools in the state. He has had more victories than any high school, college, or professional football coach in the history of the United States, and he has led his teams to ten state championships and twenty-six regional titles. I think he's one reason Summerville, South Carolina, has grown to be the town it is today.

John's impact on the players is great, but his impact on the community is fully as great.[2] He is a man whose priorities are clearly in order, and he makes certain his players also have their priorities in order. He doesn't coach football; he coaches young men. He is interested in what happens on the field, but he is far more interested in what happens off the field.

Coach McKissick's faith is deep, his loyalty to the church is strong, and his activity in the church is great. He told me that his team not only prays before the games, but they pray after the games as well. He is there to impact all phases of the young men's lives, and that's what makes him so unique. He teaches biblical qualities to the young men—qualities such as moral behavior, honesty, respect for authority, discipline, total effort, loyalty, responsibility, team play, running the race of life to win, preparing for that win. In short, here is a man who exemplifies much of what Christ taught His disciples and through the Bible has been teaching us down through the centuries.

Coach McKissick was brought up in a home where biblical principles were applied on a daily basis. He owes a large part of his coaching success to the training he received from his parents. His grandfather was a Methodist minister who preached mostly on the rural circuit, and his mother had her hands full with John and his two brothers. Though he was raised with love, devotion, and family values, he was taught right from wrong, with no in-between and no excuses.

Coach McKissick says the stories he heard and the values he learned at the family gatherings that took place every Sunday after church strongly influenced the way he has coached young men. He has tried his best to influence all of his young men in a positive manner and to teach them how to behave in a respectable way on and off the field and in the classroom. He applied Proverbs 22:6—"Train up a child in the way he should go, even when he is old he will not depart from it"—to his football team in the same way he applied it to his children. He believes that if you rear children using the moral lessons you were taught as a child and make sure they know the difference between right and wrong in all areas of life, even though they might err at times, the lessons will stay with them and they, in turn, will train their children in the same manner.

He believes that discipline, fueled by love, and a genuine concern for the young men he is working with, has played an extraordinarily significant role in his success record. Part of the way he disciplines his players is by having each young man fill out and sign the following Application for Athletic Team Membership:

I will attend practice faithfully and work as hard as I possibly can to learn the fundamentals and to develop the skills necessary for becoming a championship player. I will always conduct myself in a manner that will be a credit to my family, my school, my community, and myself.

I will try to maximize the interest in sports of others, to help players younger than myself, to encourage fair play at all times, and to respect the judgment and advice of all personnel associated with the school and the team.

I am proud to be an American and a participant in the school's athletic program. In appreciation of these privileges, I will strive to prove myself a worthy citizen and athlete. My goal will be to assist the team in being one of which everyone can be proud, a team of Champions and a Championship Team.

I hereby agree to:

1. Be neat and clean and have my hair above my ears and collar.
2. Not have evening dates prior to practice or game days.
3. Be home by 10 p.m. and in bed early before school days.
4. Never miss a practice, unless sick. If sick, I will notify one of the coaches.
5. Not be tardy for practice.
6. Be modest in attire. Good appearance is important, since athletes are always on parade.
7. Not curse.
8. Display good sportsmanship at all times.
9. Be courteous to officials.
10. Never fake an injury.
11. Not smoke or use tobacco products.
12. Not drink alcoholic beverages or use any type of illegal drug.
13. Keep in top physical condition (eating properly, working out in the weight room, etc.).

I understand that if I fail to keep my pledge, if I exhibit behavior inconsistent with my above declaration, or if I do not observe all of the foregoing standards, I will be disciplined and dropped from the team (at the discretion of the coach and the athletic director).[3]

When a young man signs the application, he is held strictly accountable—and when he complies, he is rewarded. Coach McKissick never cuts a player. If a young man shows up for practice, gives it his best shot, and follows the rules, he dresses for the game, even though the players (in most cases) and the coach understand they won't all be in the game. I kidded Coach McKissick about carrying his own cheering squad with him. You can only imagine what it does to the opposition when they see anywhere from eighty to one hundred players sitting on the benches across the field from them. Needless to say, these guys on the bench are intimidating, and their support and enthusiasm are transmitted to the field.

Coach McKissick admits that times have changed dramatically since he first started coaching and he has had to change some too. But he has stuck to his basic beliefs and has the same expectations of his players that he had back in 1952. When there are problems Coach McKissick has not been able to overcome with a player, he calls in the boy's parents for a conference. It's a comfortable meeting, because McKissick makes it a practice to stay closely in touch with each boy's parents from the beginning of his association with their child. Together they pray for God's help and direction.

McKissick says his Christian faith has sustained him and gotten him past the losses and led him to the next victory. He says he has striven to be successful in his coaching career, knowing that his faith in God and pleasing Him is his ultimate goal and his success counts for nothing without that. One verse he aspires to fulfill is 2 Timothy 4:7, in which the apostle Paul says, "I have fought the good fight, I have finished the course, I have kept the faith."

When there have been down times in McKissick's life, both personal and career, he trusts the promises of Isaiah 40:31, which says, "Those who wait on the LORD shall renew their strength; they shall mount up with wings like eagles, they shall run and not be weary, they shall walk and not faint" (NKJV).

Working as a football coach, where everything is about winning or losing, has made McKissick especially fond of Matthew 6:34:

"Do not worry about tomorrow; for tomorrow will care for itself. Each day has enough trouble of its own." If that verse can be embraced, peace and patience will not be far behind. He says coaches must be fully aware that they may be "a hero today, but a goat tomorrow."

So how much longer is he going to coach? McKissick answers that question by patiently deferring to Matthew 6:34 again, saying that he takes care of his health and hopes for the best one day at a time.

In case you are wondering if Coach McKissick wins so many games because he has a direct line to heaven, let me quote him as saying, "I also know that I can't pray to win a certain game because I don't expect God to choose which coach He wants to win and which one He wants to lose. However, I pray that we will play as hard as we can using the fundamentals we've been taught and that we'll play with good sportsmanship and be free of injuries." Coach McKissick even prays fair! It's no wonder he has been blessed so abundantly and that he has won the respect of people in Summerville and the state of South Carolina—and, for that matter, the whole football world.

John McKissick is truly a role model, not only to other coaches but to the players he has coached over the years. Those players have become educators, law enforcement officers, preachers, and businesspeople, among many other professions. These former players are now modeling the biblical principles John McKissick taught them, and they in turn are positively affecting many other lives.

When a man spends the vast majority of his life in one field of endeavor as John McKissick has, it is truly a tribute to his character when others recognize that the job that defines him has never been his first priority. Bobby Bowden, coach for Florida State University said, "I think Coach McKissick's longevity is due to the fact that he has his priorities in order and that football is not his number one priority. A man must have persistence and love of the game and love of life to coach so long."

I hope and pray John McKissick keeps on keeping on. He's already patiently coached three generations of Summerville families. With his track record, training the fourth generation should be a snap!

TONY EVANS

Preach the word; be ready in season and out of season; reprove, rebuke, exhort, with great patience and instruction.

—2 TIMOTHY 4:2

President Bush has identified Tony Evans, pastor of Oak Cliff Bible Fellowship, as a national model for faith-based reform. Dr. Evans is truly a spellbinding preacher of the gospel of Jesus Christ. He preaches from his heart and a very keen intellectual, well-educated mind, with a patient compassion for those who have encountered some of life's most difficult challenges.

Dr. Evans started Oak Cliff Bible Fellowship with ten people who met in his home for a Bible study in 1976. It wasn't long before there were twenty-seven members of the church—most of them friends, acquaintances, and family members of the Evanses. The church's growth was steady, despite the fact that it was in an economically stagnant South Dallas neighborhood.

Today, Oak Cliff Bible Fellowship numbers more than seven thousand members and is one of the nation's fastest-growing Bible churches. Dr. Evans calls the church a "laboratory for testing theological ideas about community renewal." He says that while government programs are solutions from above, "we offer solutions from alongside."[5]

Results have been spectacular. In 2002, the church helped more than three hundred members find jobs—and in his community, a job means the restoration of the self-image and pride of the working individual. It brings about family stability and reduction of crime, and when job training is provided (which Dr. Evans's church does) along with personal counseling as they deal with the total well-being of the individual, it improves the entire neighborhood. Dr. Evans points out that the church is a hospital for the sick, and he deals with things in a truly patient, loving, dynamic way. In addition, Oak Cliff Bible Fellowship's community service programs provided for more than four hundred families in 2006.

An article by Candi Cushman in the April 21, 2001, issue of *World* magazine revealed that Dr. Evans has great empathy with the people in this inner-city community.[6] Evans was raised in a similar area in Baltimore, Maryland. He became the third African American student to enroll in Dallas Theological Seminary and the first to graduate with a doctorate. He wanted to minister in the inner city because, as he says, "I'm not into doing things because they've always been done a certain way. I'm into what works. What's effective." What's effective isn't always popular, and Oak Cliff Bible Fellowship's church discipline policy is a case in point.

Pastor Evans, however, believes that God's way is always the best way. In his own family, this principle was put to the supreme test, and Pastor Evans and his church passed with flying colors. At age eighteen, his oldest daughter, Chrystal, was pregnant and unmarried. Based on Matthew 18, Oak Cliff Bible Fellowship's policy requires church members involved in divisive sin such as an extramarital affair to confess it to one another and, if necessary, the entire church. So the Evans family went before the congregation to confess the sin. "It was important for people to see our family being honest and not hiding anything," says Pastor Evans. Today, thirty-year-old Chrystal has a healthy twelve-year-old child, a successful accounting career, and is happily married.

Pastor Evans knows in his heart that honest acknowledgement of sin gives church social programs an edge over their government counterparts. He explains that to change their behavior, people have to be able to distinguish between right and wrong, and the last few years we have been taught a philosophy that is contrary to everything that God teaches, namely that whatever is right in your eyes is right and things are relative. Pastor Evans knows better. "So through discipline we say, 'this lifestyle is wrong, this lifestyle is going to hinder your progress.'"

Pastor Evans notes that his church outreach programs are firm in their Christian worldview. "To ask faith-based organizations to dichotomize their faith from their social service—that is an impossibility. The clear question ought to be, 'Are we achieving the social goals effectively for which the program has been established?'" Evans argues that the separation of church and state should never mean the separation of God and good works.[7]

I have had the privilege of knowing Tony and Lois Evans for many years, and I have worked with their daughter Priscilla and her husband, Jerry Shirer. I was even privileged to give the charge at their nuptial dinner, challenging them to follow their parents and most of all Christ in their relationship with each other. I'm pleased to say that Priscilla and Jerry periodically speak for Ziglar, Inc. and represent us well. Not only is their talent considerable, but their commitment and compassion for others are awesome.

Tony Evans is a pastor who takes the Word of God literally, and that's the reason he is involved in so many projects today. Take for example, Matthew 25:31–40:

> But when the Son of Man comes in His glory, and all the angels with Him, then He will sit on His glorious throne. All the nations will be gathered before Him; and He will separate them from one another, as the shepherd separates the sheep from the goats; and He will put the sheep on His right, and the goats on the left. Then the King will say to those on His right, 'Come, you who are blessed of My Father, inherit the kingdom prepared for you from the foundation of the

world. 'For I was hungry, and you gave Me something to eat; I was thirsty, and you gave Me something to drink; I was a stranger, and you invited Me in; naked, and you clothed Me; I was sick, and you visited Me; I was in prison, and you came to Me.' Then the righteous will answer Him, 'Lord, when did we see You hungry, and feed You, or thirsty, and give You something to drink? 'And when did we see You a stranger, and invite You in, or naked, and clothe You? 'When did we see You sick, or in prison, and come to You?' The King will answer and say to them, 'Truly I say to you, to the extent that you did it to one of these brothers of Mine, even the least of them, you did it to Me."

Along those very lines, Oak Cliff Bible Fellowship hosts church development conferences that have provided important training for more than a thousand other churches to date. The church has adopted more than sixty-five public schools in an outreach program called Project Turnaround, which provides mentoring, tutoring, and family support services for students. The church is also very strong in racial reconciliation. Acts 17:26 clearly says we are all "one blood," so that person seated next to you in church, whether black or white or anything in between, is literally a blood brother or sister.

In a November 9, 2003, article in *The Dallas Morning News*, columnist William McKenzie gives a glowing report of what happened when President Bush visited Oak Cliff Bible Fellowship. A "social entrepreneur" is how President Bush described his friend Dr. Tony Evans when talking about the church's Project Turnaround initiative. The columnist observed, "White evangelicals and black congregations may seem incongruous. . . . It's time to say hello to a force that could transform American culture and politics—if the two grasp their potential." I'm seeing this happen more and more and more.

When President Bush strode into the church service of Oak Cliff Bible Fellowship on October 29, 2003, the crowd went wild with enthusiasm. To be honest, their motivation was extraordinarily high before the president arrived. Ministers were urging the crowd to "go crazy for the Lord," shouts of "Glory, hallelujah!" echoed through the sanctuary. All the while, people clapped, swayed, and sang. Perhaps that's why a Pew Research Center poll revealed that "White evangelicals and African-American churchgoers share many beliefs. They tend to agree about Israel's fulfilling biblical prophecy about Christ's return. They think religious values should influence politics."[8]

Many comments made by the members of the church reflect the effectiveness of what Pastor Evans and his church are doing. Oak Cliff Bible Fellowship sponsors a hundred ministries actively spreading the gospel and helping people right where they are.

The patient, consistent work of Pastor Tony Evans to spread the biblical principles he teaches, preaches, and lives is one of the reasons I'm optimistic about the role Christianity can play in America today if we all start doing things God's way!

JIM DAWSON

So, as those who have been chosen of God, holy and beloved, put on a heart of compassion, kindness, humility, gentleness and patience.

—COLOSSIANS 3:12

Jim Dawson's life serves as a great example of how following biblical principles and being blessed with the fruit of patience can contribute to a beautiful family and an outstanding business career. It was obvious even to the casual observer that the Dawson family was incredibly close. He was surrounded by his six children, four of whom lived within a few hundred yards of him and one son who lived at home. Let's look at what made the late Jim Dawson a remarkable man.

Jim committed his life to Christ as a young man. When he went to work for Zebco Fishing Tackle Company, many of the executives were a little nervous, some even quite unhappy about the approach he took. But he was in the process of not only saving the company and preventing it from moving overseas for manufacturing, but also building it into a $720 million business through both internal growth and acquisitions.

When he arrived at Zebco, many of the executives and all of the workers were unaware that the company was in deep trouble. The Asian market was manufacturing fishing reels faster and of a better quality than the Zebco product. They were selling at a lower price while Zebco's products were getting more expensive every day. Inflation was high and there was no effective cost-reduction program.

Jim Dawson understood that something had to be done, and he knew it required the cooperation of every worker there. He patiently started having six-on-one meetings—six workers and him. Time after time in these meetings, he shared his vision and his dreams and told the workers that he desperately needed their input for the company to survive. After all, they were working on the line and knew far more about how to reduce costs, save time, and improve quality. They were given the freedom to make comments and observations—and Jim found them to be extraordinarily helpful. Meeting by meeting, Jim was building faith, trust, and relationships. He spent about two hours with each group, getting to know each of his workers personally. As a result, they came to respect him and believe in what he was doing.

The employees recognized Jim as someone who cared. They were impressed that he understood that people at all levels of the company needed to be aware of the necessity of change and that they wanted total honesty and clarity from management.

One of Jim's most innovative and effective procedure changes occurred late one afternoon when he spoke one-on-one with a group of company secretaries. He told them to arrive at seven thirty the next morning, remove all the Reserved parking signs, and then park their cars in the reserved spaces. When the senior managers arrived at 8 a.m., there would be no open spaces. Needless to say, the secretaries all arrived early and were delighted to fill the spaces. That day, reserved parking became a program called "The President's Club." The special places were now for anyone who had 100 percent attendance—line worker or manager. Jim turned what had been a status symbol into a motivational program for everyone.

Next, he decided to remove time clocks from the factory. He felt that these were simply another barrier between managers and employees and a stark sign of a lack of trust. One morning, he arrived at the bank of time clocks with a crowbar and began ripping them from the walls. When the workers arrived, they were surprised to see the heap of broken time clocks on the floor, the snapped electrical conduits, and the unpainted silhouettes on the walls where the time clocks had been. His message to the workers was clear and simple: We trust you to be on time and to be responsible for your hours. You will be treated no differently from the managers.

Then Jim took the process a step further: he modeled new standards for his management team. One executive realized that Jim wasn't the only person responsible for being sure there were no double standards—managers had the same responsibility.

Jim's patient actions improved his relationship and credibility with the workers. They would have walked through fire for him because he demonstrated that he really did care about equality in the plant and was willing to forego his own perks, such as the convenient reserved parking space.

All of this was designed to build support for his frame that "Zebco is in trouble." Once the above had been accomplished, Jim realized he needed an eye-opener to really get everybody working together. He did this with a persuasive demonstration.

One morning, soon after everyone arrived at the plant, all the lights in the factory were unexpectedly turned off. It was pitch-black. Then the national anthem began to play over the speaker system. When the lights were turned back on, Jim and his management team began to pass out American flags to everyone. On every flag was a small sticker that said, *Made in Taiwan*. Next, they handed out red, white, and blue smocks with the words "Zebco Quality Control Department" printed on the back. This was the day that the regular inspectors were made assemblers again, and everyone became an inspector.

Then, from the factory floor, Jim began to talk. The extinguished lights, he said, signified what would eventually happen to Zebco due to foreign competition if things didn't change. Like the American flags they held in their hands, fishing tackle would all be made in another country like Taiwan, so the company would be forced to move its production overseas and the American Zebco plants would close. He had their undivided attention.

The *Made in Taiwan* stickers made the point with brutal eloquence. If Americans no longer cared that their flags were made by foreigners, would they feel any differently about their fishing gear? He made it crystal clear that the owners could either keep Zebco going or they could sell it. Then he walked each group through the cycle of Zebco's costs, from producing the reels to selling them and explained why some reel production had already been sent to Mexico. He showed how Zebco's production costs were much higher than production costs in foreign countries. He displayed newspaper ads that showed the actual sales prices of Zebco reels versus the competition and used only a few key statistics to make his point.

Jim Dawson had patiently taken the time to build relationships with the people who would ultimately be responsible for the success of the company. He had spoken to their deep pride in their country and their strong feelings about keeping jobs in America. This was shared ground. He made it easy for the workforce to join him in the Herculean effort before them.

There is more to the story, but within fifteen years Jim and his workers increased the size of Zebco threefold, despite fierce competition from Asian companies. Then they added bicycles, camping, and marine accessories to the line. Production efficiencies increased threefold and costs dropped. The Zebco 33, which was their "bread and butter" reel that sold for $29.95 in 1954, sells as low as $9.95 in stores today. In 1991 Zebco won the Wal-Mart Vendor of the Year Award, distinguishing the firm as exceptional among Wal-Mart's eight thousand suppliers. Then in 1992, Zebco made history by winning this distinguished award for two consecutive years.[9]

Jim Dawson's heart revealed the fact that what he was doing

every step of the way was simply following biblical principles of caring for others, following the Golden Rule, and working "as to the Lord" (Ephesians 6:7).

Jim's business success opened the door for him to speak from many different platforms. Because he believed strongly in the Great Commission, he accepted as many speaking invitations as possible and he let his hosts know that, regardless of the audience, he would share the gospel of Jesus Christ in a bold and clear way. This was part of his ministry, and many state meetings found out that he offered no apology for the presentation.

Jim also donated 100 percent of his income from speaking to Shepherd's Hand Foundation, Inc., a nonprofit corporation he started to help struggling single mothers. Jim said the opportunity to present the ministry of the Shepherd's Hand Foundation and the gospel of Jesus Christ was available everywhere he spoke, and the people were open to hearing about both. Shepherd's Hand has expanded from Oklahoma into Mexico and since 1995 has averaged eighty-five students on college scholarships that pay all tuition and transportation.

Jim's presentations included sound advice for business success. People wanted to hear what a man who started as a $1.52 per hour worker and ended up as the president of a group of outdoor recreation companies with sales over $720 million had to say. To give you some examples of Jim Dawson's effectiveness as a speaker and as a witness for Christ, at a mayor's luncheon in Kansas, 121 businessmen and -women indicated they had prayed to receive Christ. At a business luncheon in Oklahoma City, 67 indicated they had prayed to receive Christ. At a leadership breakfast in Chattanooga, Tennessee, 232 people indicated they had prayed to receive Him. At a coaches' breakfast for the Fellowship of Christian Athletes with 150 coaches present, 50 indicated they had received Christ.

The list goes on and on, but the main point is that businesspeople in responsible positions can speak more openly about their faith than we sometimes think. Jim Dawson became president of his company in 1989 and grew the company to triple its size within three years. He said, "I had told many about Jesus, had become very outspoken about my relationship with Him. It never once presented a problem and it was never questioned. People knew who I was and what I stood for, and it was good."

We need to open our eyes and boldly speak about our faith like Jim Dawson did. Each of us interacts daily with people who need to be ministered to, but we often miss the opportunity in our impatience to rush on to our next appointment. The message Jim modeled for us is a message every Christian in America needs to listen to carefully. There are many people who are hurting and in need of Jesus. We need to share the best news of all in a loving, patient, carefully thought-out, and effective way.

CHAPTER 5

KINDNESS

Now for this very reason also, applying all diligence, in your faith supply moral excellence, and in your moral excellence, knowledge, and in your knowledge, self-control, and in your self-control, perseverance, and in your perseverance, godliness, and in your godliness, brotherly kindness, and in your brotherly kindness, love.

—2 Peter 1:5–7

Webster's definition of *kindness* is "good will; benevolence; that temper or disposition which delights in contributing to the happiness of others, which is exercised cheerfully in gratifying their wishes, supplying their wants or alleviating their distress; benignity of nature. *Kindness* ever accompanies love."[1]

Kindness is an outward expression of the inward fruit of love. Transformed Christians reflect the character of Jesus in that they are gracious and filled with kindness, mercy, and compassion.

Dr. Kenneth Cooper, Gary and Diane Heavin, and the late Mary Kay Ash are good examples of love and kindness. Interestingly, all four of them have been in the business of helping people feel better: Dr. Cooper and Gary and Diane Heavin through improving health through physical fitness, and Mary Kay Ash through skin care and cosmetics. Each of them understood that the only way to truly feel good and be totally healthy is to change the body spiritually from the inside out. At home, at work, and in the marketplace, they kindly shared the love and the saving grace of Jesus Christ with others, leaving the results to God.

KENNETH H. COOPER

*Let us run with endurance the race that is set before us,
fixing our eyes on Jesus, the author and perfecter of faith.*
—HEBREWS 12:1–2

By any measurement it is safe to say that Dr. Kenneth Cooper has had an impact on the health of the world. He has lectured in more than fifty countries and has received many honors from around the world. He is a pioneer in the medical field who decided it would be far more practical and beneficial to keep people well and healthy than only treating those with serious health problems. Personally, Dr. Cooper has been tremendously helpful to me. I had been overweight for many years when I began following his guidelines and lost weight in 1973. More than thirty years later, that weight is still gone and I still go to his clinic regularly for checkups.

Dr. Cooper met many challenges on the way to becoming a world-renowned physician because the medical profession was not ready to hear what he had to say. Fortunately, those of us who aspired to live healthy lives and achieve all we could accomplish were ready. He is a man of deep faith, and that faith is evident in his marriage, professional, and family life because each area of his life is based on biblical principles.

Dr. Cooper has always been involved in community affairs and even now, in his midseventies, seems to have ample energy for working long hours and performing at top capacity. As a younger man, his ability in track approached the Olympic level and he has carried that level of performance achievement into every area in which he has participated.

The direction of Dr. Cooper's life became evident as he pursued information on how to help people live healthier lives. He has always put God first, family second, and career third. He feels many people were placed in his life providentially, which is another reason his faith remains so strong.

Today he shakes his head in amazement at where his career has led him. In 1970, at almost forty years of age, he resigned his commission from the United States Air Force with the intent to move full-time into the field of preventive medicine in the private sector. With a pregnant wife, a five-year-old daughter, no health insurance, and no savings to speak of, leaving the security of the military and moving to a new community where he was essentially unknown took great faith and a lot of prayers. He and his wife, Millie, prayed fervently about the decision, that it would be the correct one and that it would glorify God.

He moved to Dallas and set up his initial office with only three people on staff. About a year later, Dr. Cooper's clinic moved to the property that he acquired because of his friend Joe McKinney and, as he put it, with the help of providential blessings that came his way. It's easy to understand why Dr. Cooper shakes his head in wonder—he now has more than 550 employees on his staff, including twenty-three MDs, seventeen who see patients for comprehensive physical examinations, three radiologists, two cardiologists, and one dentist.

Despite some strong opposition from the established medical community who thought his idea of prevention through exercise, primarily walking and jogging, had not been thoroughly tested, Dr. Cooper overcame all of the objections. The extent of his philosophy has no boundaries. In some countries, particularly in Central and South America, they even have another name for jogging: they call it "Coopering"!

In addition to Dr. Cooper's outstanding professional career, he enjoys a solid relationship with his wife, Millie, who has been a big supporter over the years. Millie continues to be a big encouragement and is herself an excellent speaker; periodically, they conduct seminars together.

In spite of his busy career doing what he loves to do, Dr. Cooper has always been careful to set aside time to be with his family. They have a son and a daughter, of whom they are very proud—and justly so. He is also very active in his church, thanks to his Christian mother and his grandmother, whom he credits with having the greatest impact on his life with Christ. He gives God the credit for what he has been able to do in his career. In many ways, you could say that Dr. Cooper is a Renaissance man, having done a variety of things during his undergraduate days to help him develop a keen interest in people, nature, and what our incredible country has to offer.

In nearly all of his presentations, Dr. Cooper refers to his Christian faith and biblical values. And as a practicing physician, he tries to use biblical principles in working and counseling with patients, particularly those who are having physical, emotional, or financial problems. This is where the fruit of his kindness shows most. So few physicians refer their patients to the Supreme Healer, the true source of all power and strength. But Dr. Cooper likes to refer those who are anxious to Matthew 6:27: "Who of you by being worried can add a single hour to his life?" Another verse he frequently refers to is 2 Corinthians 4:8, which says, "We are pressed on every side by troubles, but not crushed and broken. We are perplexed because we don't know why things happen as they do, but we don't give up and quit" (TLB). As a follow-up to that verse, he'll add the last part of 2 Corinthians 4:18, "The troubles will soon be over, but the joys to come will last forever" (TLB).

Dr. Cooper uses his Bible not only for his personal meditations, but for guidance in his professional life and in counseling his patients. Nearly every morning of the week, he spends at least fifteen minutes in prayer and Bible study. He prays daily for President George Bush and a list of patients, friends, and family members. I'm positive that if more doctors prayed for their patients, they'd see a better end result of their care and efforts. Dr. Cooper also reads religious books, including those by Chuck Swindoll and Max Lucado. He believes, and I concur, that to enjoy life to the fullest, you must be both spiritually and physically fit.

Kenneth Cooper told me that if I'd asked him thirty-seven years ago what he would be doing in 2007, he would have missed it "a thousandfold." He says his vision was finite, but the Lord's was infinite. He won't even hazard a guess as to what will happen in the remaining years of his life!

Dr. Cooper's life displays the truth of one of his favorite sayings: "If you turn loose and let God have control of your life, He will amaze you as to what will happen!"

GARY AND DIANE HEAVIN

Or do you not know that your body is a temple of the Holy Spirit who is in you, whom you have from God, and that you are not your own? For you have been bought with a price: therefore glorify God in your body.
—1 Corinthians 6:19–20

A s those of you who have heard me speak or read my books know, I believe simple clarity is the best approach to life. Out of clarity come innovation and the trust of the people you are working with. What biblical principle could be more simple and yet more profound than "God is love" (1 John 4:8)?

I met a man in 2003 who believes with all his heart that God is love, Christ is Lord, the Bible is the perfect guidebook for life, and the Golden Rule (backed up with the Ten Commandments) is the best and most creative approach to life and success. A clearly simplistic and profoundly sound way to live.

Gary Heavin invited me to speak at his and his wife's company's national convention in Las Vegas after his brother heard me speak freely about my faith in a presentation. Gary wanted me to follow the same approach at his event, and the results were extraordinary. We are now working together in a very exciting way. Gary has a passion for life, a love for his fellow man, and the love and business partnership of his wife, Diane—together they make an incredible team.

The company Gary and Diane founded is Curves International, a fitness club franchise that is one of the most successful stories in the business world. Curves International implements an approach to life and health that has revolutionized many lives and has set the franchise world on fire. Curves grew to more than six thousand franchises in less than one-fourth the time it took McDonald's and Subway to reach that number. Today they are concentrating on foreign markets. The Curves exercise program has inspired more than four million women who are exercising regularly in Curves facilities. Two of those women are my wife and my daughter-in-law, and they share my enthusiasm for the company.

In 1976, Gary Heavin dropped out of a premed program to take over a failing health and fitness club. He, with the help of his brother, drove it to success, ultimately opening fourteen women's fitness centers over a ten-year period. By age twenty-six, Gary was a millionaire. But unwise business decisions led to a $5 million debt, bankruptcy, and the loss of his homes, plane, cars, everything. But those same decisions also led him to commit his life to Christ. In the despair that followed his great loss, Gary Heavin was driven to his knees in prayer and learned, like so many before him, that God does answer knee-mail.

Heavin likes to say, "God showed me how to handle poverty, and He's shown me how to handle wealth." He believes with all of his heart that he had to go through what he went through to be where he is today. His first serious life trial was the loss of his mother when he was only thirteen years old. She had suffered from depression, was overweight, and had high blood pressure. He believes her death has been the driving force behind his lifelong passion for women's health and that a fitness program like Curves might have saved her.

Curves is focused on creating a community of support specifically designed for women. The workout is easy to follow, lasts only thirty minutes, and is available to women at their appropriate level of effort.

Gary and Diane have spent millions of dollars validating the effectiveness of the Curves program. Research through Baylor University's

Women's Health and Fitness Initiative has given proof to the skeptics that three thirty-minute workouts a week on their specially designed equipment, combined with their nutritional programs, enable the club member to attain and maintain her ideal weight.[2]

Curves members receive tremendous encouragement and direction that enables them to gain strength as well. Gary's simple thirty-minute program of moving from one machine to another exercises all parts of the body and includes aerobic activity, stretching, and strength training, which is the missing ingredient in many exercise and nutritional programs. An unexpected but welcome benefit of Curves membership is the friendships women establish. The machines are set up in a circle so the women can see each other and talk as they work out. Many of these women have told me that they have built closer relationships with more people in a few months at Curves than they had been able to do in their lifetimes.

Gary acknowledges that on occasion he has lost business because he is so open in his Christian faith, but he consistently makes his faith known in his company. Because this is America, if they desire to do so, franchise owners can exercise their own faith, whatever it might be, right there in the facilities. With kindness, Gary lets them know up front that he is going to be talking about his faith. Many of his franchise owners of other religious preferences state that they appreciate and share many of Gary's values.

At a recent convention in Toronto, Gary told the audience of his franchise owners that he was going to reduce the "take," which, incidentally, was already well below half of the monthly royalty the typical franchiser charges, because it was disproportionate to the franchisees in small population areas. Price increases are common; it takes an uncommon man to reduce his income so that others can prosper. Gary and Diane want to help others succeed, and their kindness is evidence of that desire.

God has blessed Gary and Diane to an incredible degree. They fervently believe that if you seek first the kingdom of God and his righteousness, all other things will fall in place (Matthew 6:33). They give far more than 10 percent of their personal income to their church and other charities, and with the support of their franchise owners and club members, they have raised more than fifty million pounds of food for local food banks in the last decade. This is done in March because most food banks do well at Thanksgiving and Christmas, but the pantries are often bare by March. So Gary and Diane give at a time when the need is greatest, an idea that was born out of their God-given kindness.

How is Curves doing compared to other franchises? In just over ten years, they have become the sixth largest franchise company in America and the ninth largest in the world. It's continually ranked the number one fitness franchise and over the last five years has been ranked as the world's fastest-growing franchise, the number one low-investment franchise, and among the top three best franchises in America.

A simple approach to health and fitness, presented by a man and woman who are doing things God's way, has benefited them, their franchisees, and Curves members. Who can question the success of that?

MARY KAY ASH

Do not let kindness and truth leave you;
Bind them around your neck,
Write them on the tablet of your heart.

—PROVERBS 3:3

When Mary Kay Ash founded her cosmetics company, she wanted to create something that would give women a real opportunity for career stability and growth. She had experienced discrimination (the opposite of kindness) in her own career, so she was totally committed to demonstrating kindness to women by making positive changes for women in the business world.

Before she started Mary Kay Cosmetics, on at least two different occasions Mary Kay trained men who were later promoted over her. When she started Mary Kay Cosmetics, she determined she would do it differently and initiated a philosophy that was effective and innovative.

From the beginning, she taught that she wanted her consultants and directors to put God first, family second, and Mary Kay Cosmetics third in order of priority. This put the lives of the women in the organization in proper perspective.

Benefiting from the leadership of Mary Kay and her son, who was a truly remarkable marketing administrator, Mary Kay Cosmetics has experienced phenomenal growth. The signature Mary Kay pink automobiles can be seen not only in every city in America, but in places around the world. When you talk to a Mary Kay representative, you discover someone who is genuinely excited and grateful for the opportunity she has been given. Not only are Mary Kay representatives generally committed, loyal, and devoted to the company and its products, but their income is off the charts in the world of sales.

Mary Kay learned the hard way what John J. Eagan of American Cast Iron Pipe Company had always known: if you sell your company stock, you lose control of the way your business is conducted. Mary Kay took her company public—and then had to buy it all back at an incredible cost when it was apparent that the company was no longer going to be run the way she had intended it to be run: with Christ at the center.

I had the privilege of being a close friend of Mary Kay Ash, and her kindness played a major role in my career when she opened the door for me to speak to her consultants and directors. She invited me to address regional meetings all across the nation as well as national meetings on several occasions. For that kindness I have always been grateful.

Mary Kay used what she was blessed with to bless others. Her husband, Mel, died of cancer in 1980, and the experience of witnessing his physical pain and grieving his death prompted her to found the Mary Kay Ash Charitable Foundation in 1996. The foundation funds scientific research with the goal of ending cancers that primarily target women. The foundation also promotes a program called Break the Silence™, which brings attention to domestic violence and contributes millions to women's shelters annually.

Because of Mary Kay's Christian faith, countless numbers of her employees were the beneficiaries of her extraordinary kindness. Many of her deeds of kindness and generosity were done in private, according to the biblical principle of giving to others out of God's kindness, not to draw attention to oneself. The best legacy of all is that many people will spend eternity in heaven because of Mary Kay Ash's influence on their lives.

CHAPTER 6

GOODNESS

Walk as children of Light (for the fruit of the Light con-
sists in all goodness and righteousness and truth), trying
to learn what is pleasing to the Lord.

—Ephesians 5:8–10

The third outward fruit is goodness. The goodness of, or generosity of, the true believer is apparent to others. Goodness in this sense refers to the generous nature that comes from understanding that what is yours is God's first. Christians share from a place of abundance, knowing they cannot outgive God. When prompted to give, whether it be of their time, their money, or other assets, Christians respond from the heart.

The fruit of goodness abounds in the stories of Butch Davis, Mary Crowley, and Jim Norman. Butch Davis, as a football coach, is a leader of men—while Mary Crowley, who founded Home Interiors and Gifts, was a leader of women. As a business consultant, Jim Norman works with both men and women. Each of these individuals set wonderful examples of what it is to put Christ first and they made themselves available. Read on to discover how their actions influenced the lives of others.

BUTCH DAVIS

Let us not lose heart in doing good, for in due time we will reap if we do not grow weary. So then, while we have opportunity, let us do good to all people.

—GALATIANS 6:9–10

For many years the University of Miami's Hurricane football team was going nowhere. Then Coach Howard Schnellenberger brought the university football fame, leading them to the national championship in 1983. Since then the team has been coached by Jimmy Johnson, Dennis Erickson, Butch Davis, Larry Coker, and now Randy Shannon. All have won championships except Butch Davis. However, the success of the 2001 team under Larry Coker was a reflection of the recruiting efforts of Butch Davis and his coaching staff and the creation of an environment conducive to success.

The May 21, 2003, issue of *USA Today* reported that the Atlantic Coast Conference was courting the Miami Hurricanes heavily because they knew they were a big draw and would add money to the coffers of all the ACC teams.[1] It was a glowing tribute about the Hurricanes football team, but the article neglected to mention what happened to turn them around and make their presence so highly desirable. I'll fill in what they left out.

When Butch Davis took over the team in 1995, its reputation was shot. Goodness of the virtuous sort was nowhere to be seen. The team's behavior in soundly beating the University of Texas in the 1991 Cotton Bowl, during which they incurred 16 penalties for 202 yards and used a lot of trash talk, had put them in a bad light. When they played Notre Dame, some enterprising fellow created a

T-shirt that read *Catholics vs. Criminals* that sold like hotcakes. A number of the Hurricanes' players were frequently in trouble with the law. When they played Penn State for the national championship, they showed up in battle fatigues. Though they were favored to win—they lost. I'm convinced that on this neutral site the crowd's support for Penn State made the difference.

Coach Davis started making changes by doing things right. He took an interest in his players that went far beyond the normal responsibilities of coaching. He gave the team a fresh image by stressing moral virtue and the importance of character, integrity, academics, and community involvement. He prepared his players to win football games by preparing them to win in life, a skill he is qualified to teach because he knows the One who gives us life more abundantly (John 10:10).

Several years ago Butch Davis attended my company's Born to Win seminar in Dallas. When that particular seminar is over, I announce something along the lines of, "Many of you have inquired about what happened to me on July 4, 1972. In a separate room in ten minutes I'm going to share what happened. All of you are invited; all of you are welcome. Not all of you are expected to attend." At that session, Butch Davis committed his life to Christ.

Two years later I played golf with Butch in Miami, and he told me that every Monday morning he, his assistant coaches, and staff were in Bible study—and that, on average, fifty-five of his players participated in the Fellowship of Christian Athletes and attended church services before each game. He believes that when the times get tough and the game is on the line, character is an important factor in determining the eventual winner. His team's record speaks for itself.

During his first year as coach of the Hurricanes, Coach Davis suspended several players and made it clear that behavior detrimental to the success of the team and the players would not be tolerated. Many of the locals were not thrilled about the suspensions, but it became known that a new regime had taken over. In 1995, the team finished the season 8–3, followed by 9–3 in 1996, and 5–6 in 1997, having lost thirty-one scholarships due to NCAA sanctions because of recruiting violations before his tenure. In 1998 and 1999 they won 9–3, followed by 11–1 in 2000 when they were denied the spot in the national championship game. The radical improvements came because quality athletes from all over the country recognized that Coach Davis and his staff were individuals of faith and character who gave generously of themselves to enhance the lives of their players, and players of moral virtue started attending the University of Miami to be part of the "new" tradition.

Butch Davis resigned as coach of the Hurricanes in January 2001 after winning the Sugar Bowl by beating Florida 37–20. The team he and his staff recruited won the national championship in 2002.

In the year 2001, Coach Davis accepted an offer from the Cleveland Browns and took the same character-based philosophy with him. It was the Browns' third year with the National Football League, and they finished with an improved 7–9 season. Coach Davis went 24–35 with the Browns before resigning in 2004. He then worked in broadcasting for two seasons before signing as head coach of the University of North Carolina in November 2006.

Butch tells me that after only four months at the University of North Carolina, he has seen an amazing transformation in the attitude and in the spirit of the football players, thanks in large part to the great assistant coaching staff. Coach Davis also says the Monday morning Bible study is enjoying the biggest turnout it has ever had, tripling in attendance in a short amount of time. He sees God at work in the lives of his players and in the football program overall.

Living by and teaching biblical principles has had a profound effect on Coach Davis and the people he comes in contact with. Butch says that Psalms 23 and 121 comfort him when the times get tough or when he has been on the road and away from home a great deal. The thoughts expressed on courage in Joshua 1 help when he is facing adversity. From an uplifting point of view, when Butch considers the sacrifices he makes for his wife and son, he is reminded that there is no greater sacrifice than the one we read about in John 3:16.

Success really is sweetest when it is gained with the goodness, integrity, truth, and love Christ has taught us.

MARY CROWLEY

*Do not neglect doing good and sharing, for with such
sacrifices God is pleased.*

—HEBREWS 13:16

Mary Crowley was truly one of the most remarkable people I've
ever known. She was strong in her faith, generous in her contributions, and unique in her approach to many different things. She
founded Home Interiors and Gifts on a limited amount of money.
Most bankers refused to consider granting her a loan because of her
"revolutionary" ideas, which were based on moral virtue. She
believed suppliers should be paid when they presented the bill, not
carried on the books for thirty, sixty, or ninety days as many businesses did.

Mary built her company on biblical principles and initiated a
process that gave opportunity to the people who displayed and sold
the products. The fairly priced home decorating items were beautiful, useful, and practical. Using the book of Proverbs as her guide
for teaching her managers biblical principles, she conducted training classes in tranquil surroundings, away from the hubbub of too
much activity.

She literally contributed millions of dollars in scholarship funds
to Christian colleges and undoubtedly saved at least two of those
colleges with her kindness and generosity. The beautiful Mary C.
Crowley Chapel at the Carr P. Collins complex of the Salvation
Army in Dallas was funded by the Crowley Carter Foundation in
honor of Mary. Her interest in the spiritual health of people was
ever-present during her lifetime, and I can't think of a more fitting

tribute to remember her by than a chapel that men and women who are being restored spiritually, mentally, and physically can worship in.

Another significant contribution to society that is a part of Mary's legacy is The Mary Crowley Medical Research Center, located on the campus of the Baylor University Medical Center at Dallas. It is one of the largest patient treatment centers for gene therapy in the United States and seeks to find vaccine, gene, and cellular therapies that will expand treatment options for patients with cancer, a disease Mary battled for several years before her death.

Prior to starting Home Interiors and Gifts, Mary worked for a company where she was in charge of sales and had been largely responsible for building the organization to unprecedented heights. But when the company started serving cocktails at its conventions, she protested very strongly, recognizing the inherent danger. Consequently, because of her protests, one morning she awoke to find her desk sitting on her front porch. Because of her faith and goodness, she had been fired in the cruelest way imaginable.

Romans 8:28 assures us, "God causes all things to work together for good to those who love God, to those who are called according to His purpose." Mary Crowley proved that principle. Her photograph hangs on my "Wall of Gratitude" because she played a huge role in my life and career. Not only did Mary model the biblical principles she lived by, but she repeatedly invited me to address her organization and visit her church as I was getting started in my career.

Home Interiors and Gifts is still going strong years after Mary Crowley's death. The same biblical concepts, principles, and processes are firmly in place and are being followed because the company acknowledges that God's way is still the best way.

The year 2002 was a banner year for Home Interiors and Gifts, with over $1 billion in retail sales; 2003 was even better. One of the major reasons for the company's success is that the company ensures the displayers win, the customers win, the managers win, and the company wins. It is truly an "everyone wins" situation, so much so that in 2003, of the twelve hundred managers operating in the United States, Canada, and Mexico, only ten resigned their positions. Six of those retired, while the other four missed the quota required to maintain their manager position and are still with the company.

Since trust is the glue that holds any organization together, trust is evidenced in spades at Home Interiors and Gifts. After years of personally dealing with this company, I can tell you that what you see *is* what you get, and their word really is their bond. They apply biblical principles in all of their business practices. Bills are still paid upon receipt the way Mary Crowley insisted that they be. Their suppliers give them generous terms because they know the terms will always be met and a Home Interiors and Gifts check is always a good check.

The company makes certain all of their people have the opportunity to enjoy the "home court advantage," meaning simply they recognize the value of the spouse at home and that everything is done to benefit the family, not just the displayer or the manager.

In short, Home Interiors and Gifts is a company with a heart and a foundation based on the Word of God. Mary always lifted others up and was a more than equal opportunity employer. She was also the first woman to serve on the board of directors of the Billy Graham Evangelistic Association. Shortly after we met Mary in the early 1970s, my family and I were impressed to learn that she loved to employ mentally and physically challenged adults in every possible capacity. A unique business decision that was ahead of its time and was yet another reflection of the fruit of Mary's personal walk with Jesus Christ.

Today, Mary's legacy of generosity and goodness lives on in A Pocketful of Hope™ Charities, which was formed in response to 9/11 and raised $1 million for the American Red Cross Liberty

Disaster Relief Fund. Over the years, Home Interiors has given in excess of $65 million to a large variety of charitable causes, including Habitat for Humanity International, the American Heart Association, and the Susan G. Komen Breast Cancer Foundation.

Yes, Mary's fruit of goodness, her generosity, is still visible through her legacy and her company, though she went home to be with her Lord many years ago.

JIM NORMAN

If you continue in My word, then you are truly disciples of Mine; and you will know the truth, and the truth will make you free.

—JOHN 8:31–32

I've known Jim Norman for almost twenty-five years, and watching how God has forged him into His very own has been a journey and a blessing. I've seen Jim on top of the world and in the pit of despair—and I've seen him give up endless hours to help others who have found themselves in the same predicaments. His generosity with his time as well as his other assets has blessed many through the years. He is an obedient servant of the Lord and his goodness abounds . . . but that wasn't always the case.

Jim Norman walked the aisle of First Baptist Church of Harleton, Texas, when he was twelve years old. He was excited about getting baptized and he thought he'd be a different boy in his heart, but he wasn't. The next week he was still doing the things he'd always gotten in trouble for, so in his childish mind he determined that God didn't care enough about him to fix him. He shrugged off his disappointment and determined to do everything himself.

His father taunted and ridiculed him in an effort to "make a man of him," and Jim developed a deep resentment of anyone who had authority over him. Things went downhill at school and at home. When he was in ninth grade, Jim's dad sent him to a military academy where "they could straighten him out."

After many demerits and hours of drills, Jim began to conform. He blossomed in the military environment and learned that kudos were gratifying. He liked the honors that went with high achievement and he outwardly reformed. Yet inwardly, his heart still rebelled and his mind told him he wasn't good enough—not good enough for his father and not good enough for God.

After Jim graduated from Texas Christian University, he entered the air force as an officer with the dream of becoming a pilot. A physical revealed a problem in his eyes that kept him from flying. Gravely disappointed, Jim began a journey that took him places he wished he'd never gone.

One of those places was the Philippines, during the Vietnam War. The memories from those dark times are still heavy, and Jim avoids talking about his experiences there. The time he spent with his parents in Harleton after he was discharged from the service helped a little, but it was months before he could muster up enough energy to find a job.

Shortly after, Jim went to work in Fort Worth, Texas, and he met the woman he eventually married. Unfortunately, she was married to someone else at the time—but neither of them let that get in their way. As soon as her divorce was final, they said their "I dos."

One very successful business, one adopted stepdaughter, two children, and twelve miserable years later, they divorced. Jim and his wife had turned to alcohol to help soothe the pain of their relationship. They had even tried going to church and counseling, but it was too little, too late. There was too much distrust and fear of the future, and Jim's marriage dissolved into a battle of note among the most powerful attorneys in Fort Worth.

The day his divorce was final, Jim had his first date with Julie, the woman who would become his second wife. Three months later, they were married. He assured her he didn't need lots of time to recover from his divorce. He said he'd been emotionally divorced for years . . . but three months into the marriage Jim's drinking escalated. His stunned wife, not knowing how to respond, drank with him. The insanity continued.

However, the spiritual journey that Jim had begun in an effort to save his failed marriage continued as well. He and Julie found a church home and became very involved. In spite of the alcoholic fog they lived in, they both began to hear the Word of God and it was taking root.

After two and a half years, Jim and Julie participated in an Alcoholics Anonymous group, where they learned how to "let go and let God." Jim told God that everything he had was His and asked God to remove anything that might be a stumbling block to Jim's relationship with Him. Within three months, Jim's high-roller lifestyle came to an abrupt halt. The reasons were many and varied, but Jim knew it was as God wanted it to be.

Ultimately, Jim lost everything he owned: his house, his cars, his checking account, everything. All of the material belongings that had signified to the world that he was a "somebody" were gone. The things that propped up his ego—gone. But he was sober and happy for the first time that he could remember.

With the "things" out of his way, Jim could focus on God. For months he studied his Bible. He began sponsoring men in AA, and when "the God of their understanding" didn't make sense to them, he'd tell them about Jesus. Soon Jim was holding weekly Bible studies at his home for his AA friends who wanted to know more about the God of the Bible.

Jim started a consulting business and worked from his home. Though things seemed okay, he and his wife had not learned how to communicate after they quit drinking. Their marriage of almost twelve years was strained, and when Jim momentarily fell back into an addiction he had had to pornography, she left him.

Fortunately, Jim and Julie's church family counseled, supported, and encouraged them to save the marriage, pointing out that God hates divorce and He designed marriage to be a lifelong commitment. Jim, having been convicted by God, stopped viewing pornography on the Internet even before Julie confronted him about it. But Julie wanted a separation anyway, insisting that they needed to do something drastically different to get their marriage back on the right road.

After a year of counseling and attending church together, Jim and Julie reconciled and now have the kind of marriage God always intended for them to have. They are best friends, lovers, and confidants. Neither of them can imagine life without the other. They truly enjoy each other and tremble at the thought of what they might have missed.

Since that time, God has used Jim and Julie to help others save their marriages. Jim regularly counsels men who struggle with addiction of all kinds, teaching them to take their thoughts captive, just as the Scripture instructs. Every Saturday afternoon for several years Jim took a Bible-based AA meeting to a prison about an hour from his home. He has been blessed to run into some of the men from the prison and to learn that they are still sober and are living for Jesus outside the walls that used to confine them.

Jim has also started a weekly radio ministry called *Wise People.* Jim interviews people who live their lives for Jesus. The topics are as varied as are the people Jesus uses to do His bidding, and I can assure you the radio show is full of hope-inspiring messages. I had the pleasure of sharing my story of salvation on Jim's program some months ago.

Yes, God can take a person who loves material things and is addicted to alcohol and pornography, and heal him and use him to influence others to turn to Christ. Jim Norman has discovered the truth that sets people free—and that is good!

PART THREE

THE UPWARD FRUIT *of the* SPIRIT

CHAPTER 7

FAITHFULNESS

Well done, good and faithful slave. You were faithful with a few things, I will put you in charge of many things; enter into the joy of your master.

—MATTHEW 25:21

Through the Holy Spirit, believers are faithful and steadfast in their love and devotion.

Their faith is unchanging and reliable. Believers trust God. They believe in Him and they obey Him. And like a moth to flame, the faithful are drawn to Christ in an irresistible way.

Bill Bright, founder of Campus Crusade for Christ International, business entrepreneur Mike Godwin, and Horatio Alger winner Tom Harken are men whose lives are great examples of how to serve the Lord faithfully. Bill Bright has already received his heavenly reward.

BILL BRIGHT

I thank Christ Jesus our Lord, who has strengthened me, because He considered me faithful, putting me into service.

—1 TIMOTHY 1:12

I was upset, amazed, and disappointed when the July 22, 2003, edition of *USA Today* gave more print space to the death of Ozzy Ozbourne's black Chihuahua, Lulu, than they had to the death of Bill Bright, founder and leader of the world's largest Christian ministry, Campus Crusade for Christ International. I think that discrepancy speaks of the true condition of our society and explains to a large extent why Bill Bright was faithful for more than fifty years to fulfill what is known as the Great Commission (Matthew 28:18–20) and tell every living person on earth about Jesus Christ.

Bill died July 19, 2003, of pulmonary fibrosis, the same disease that took my daughter Suzan's life on May 13, 1995. This reminded me that Bill, like Suzan, has only just now truly begun to live. Many would say he sacrificed much for his beliefs and to prosper his ministry, but I can assure you his heavenly rewards are rich beyond our imagination.

I include Bill Bright's story in this book because his life is a model of faithfulness and biblical principles. In being obedient to the Word of God, Bill wrote a seventy-seven-word booklet titled *The Four Spiritual Laws*. To date, that booklet has been printed in all the major world languages and distributed to more than 2.5 billion people. The feature-length documentary he commissioned in 1979 on the life of Christ, *JESUS*, has been viewed by more than six billion people in

228 countries and has been translated into more than nine hundred different languages. His *Four Spiritual Laws* booklet is the most widely disseminated religious booklet in history, and the *JESUS* film is the most widely viewed and most widely translated film in history. I believe Dr. Bright's work will be carried on until the Lord returns. Souls will be saved and eternity will be richer because of his faithfulness. Success on this scale is only possible with the help of God.

Bill simply did what he was called to do and remained faithful year after year. The organization he began as an outreach to UCLA students in 1951 is now based in Orlando, Florida; has a staff of 26,000 full-time employees and 225,000 trained volunteers; and serves people in 191 countries. Originally, Campus Crusade for Christ was just that . . . a campus ministry. Today the ministry has several specialized outreach projects and ministers to people in the inner cities, prisons, governments, families, the military, business, athletics, the music business, and many others.

In 1996, forty-five years after he began his ministry, Bill Bright was awarded the world's largest annual financial award, the Templeton Prize, worth more than $1 million. And true to his faithfulness and living his life for the glory of God, he donated the proceeds of the award to training Christians in the spiritual benefits of fasting and prayer and for the fulfillment of the Great Commission.

His awards and honorary doctorates are too numerous to mention, and I'm convinced Bill didn't even keep track of them. The only number he was interested in was the number of people who were hearing about Christ and coming to know Him personally.

If you would like to further the work to which he gave his life, you can contribute to the William R. Bright Legacy Trust (account #2747894), 100 Lake Hart Drive, Orlando, FL 32832.

It's an honor and a privilege to write about a man whose life was so well lived. To God be the glory!

MIKE GODWIN

I have chosen the faithful way;
I have placed Your ordinances before me.

—PSALM 119:30

Mike Godwin was born in Valdosta, Georgia, where he lives and works to this day. He was a latchkey kid because his parents worked very hard to provide a better life for him. Fortunately, Mike attended church as a child, and though his Bible study teachers had a big impact on his life, he ultimately strayed from his early teachings.

During his college years, Mike did some things he's not particularly proud of. He observed that if you don't know what you're really after, sometimes you have to find out what you're missing before you appreciate what you've got. He got involved in alcohol, so his father pulled him out of his college fraternity and put him to work with a plumbing contractor. He wanted to be sure that Mike experienced working outside in one-hundred-degree temperatures so that he would recognize the need for an education and be motivated enough to do what was necessary to get one. Mike's father always held two or three jobs in an effort to improve the lives of his wife and children. Mike inherited that work ethic and believes that success comes with hard work—which may be why working in the heat didn't bother Mike.

He was still working as a plumber when the law in Georgia changed, requiring representatives of plumbing contractors to have a master plumber's license. Mike wanted to take the test, but his boss thought the people who had been working for him for fifteen to twenty years were better prepared to pass it. Mike was not discouraged. He told his boss he believed he could pass the test and that if he failed he would pay for the test. The boss readily agreed, probably in hopes of teaching this young "upstart" a thing or two. Well, guess what? When the test results arrived, Mike's boss called him in and said, "Son, you can't tell anybody you passed the test because everybody else here failed it, and there'll be an uprising!" However, Mike did get to drive from job to job inspecting the work of the more experienced men.

Mike eventually formed his own business by taking a subsidiary of that company off to the side in a multifamily division. The new company developed into quite a large one, with 125-plus employees working over ten to fifteen states.

Mike's ability to attract to his company good people with a strong work ethic had a huge impact on his success. Though he didn't overtly apply Christian principles to his business at that time, nor did he share his beliefs with his employees, he recognized that God was with him all the while.

Mike is a risk taker, but not a gambler. He decided that because his business had become boring, he would start another one. His mother thought he was crazy, but Mike credits his success at founding the Ambling Company—a real estate development, construction, and management firm—to his strong work ethic, lots of determination, and his trust and faith in God.

To this day, when one of Mike's employees says he or she is not happy working with him, he tells them to do themselves—and him—a favor by getting another job. He believes that a job is something you hate to go to, but work is something that is a part of you, something you enjoy. He enjoys seeing others prosper and develop as well.

Mike is grateful for the fact that he has helped others start businesses and believes that six or eight companies have been born out of his attitude and his success. He says, "I don't think you can ever go wrong by helping people be successful." He encourages his employees to work hard and to do the things they need to do to have their own businesses.

Mike confesses that he and his wife, Jayne, had a lot of material things at a young age. They were able to do things that their parents couldn't do because of their successful business, and they bought into the "keeping up with the Joneses" philosophy. Unfortunately, they had grown apart and they lived almost separately, as if she had her life and he had his.

Even though God wasn't in the center of their marriage, He was around Mike and Jayne individually. Mike had always admired the faith of his friend David Pipkin. When David invited Mike to go on an Emmaus Walk with him, he had no idea that Mike and Jayne were having marriage problems because they'd kept it secret. As Mike recalls, when he went on the Emmaus Walk, "our marriage was just about to be destroyed. I did not want to go but I went, kicking and screaming. God obviously knew what He was doing." Mike said, "The Emmaus Walk came at the right time in my life, and I was totally prepared to be broken down. I'm one of those guys who can't go halfway down the pole before he starts going back up. I've got to go down and get deep in the bottom below the ground before I can really look around and evaluate where I am. But once I come out, I'm going straight to the top—and I'm never going back."

God changed Mike's heart in a revolutionary way on the Emmaus Walk and entered his life to stay. That was many years ago, but Mike still gets emotional when he talks about that walk. "While I was gone on the Emmaus Walk, God was working on Jayne. When I came back, she immediately recognized a change in my heart. She was enthusiastic about her opportunity to take the Emmaus Walk two weeks later because she had seen how my attitude had changed. She wanted to go."

Mike is grateful that since that time, he and Jayne have enjoyed one of the finest marriages any two people could possibly have, and they work hard to keep it that way. They established checkpoints and meet quarterly to faithfully review their goals and objectives—to make sure they are being the best parents they can be and the best husband and wife they can be. They also strive to be the best Christians they can be, stating, "We check on each other and hold each other accountable." He is proud to say that Jayne is his best friend, his lover, and that they do and talk about the same things. "But most of all we have one common denominator, and that is that Jesus Christ is at the center of our marriage, our family life, and our business. He is in the center of everything—which is where He should be." The faithfulness that Mike and Jayne have is easily recognized in their personal, family, and business life.

Since the time of their Emmaus Walk, Mike and Jayne have spent many hours counseling other couples. Mike says, "When Ambling Company was started, God was at the center of everything in my life." They open their board meetings in prayer and allow their offices to be used for different women's and men's Bible studies and all types of events relative to studying God's Word.

The Godwins give to Christian-based organizations. They acknowledge God in their mission statement and in their creed, and they pray for God's grace in everything they do. Mike never refers to Ambling Company as "*my* company" but rather "*our* company," and that's the attitude he ingrains in employees.

The growth of Ambling Companies continues to be evidence of what God can do when you make Him the CEO of your company. In 2006, Ambling University Development Group, AUDG, a division of Ambling Company, was undergoing a major trial. The business plan was failing miserably and discussions about the future of the business line were occurring. It was clear to all concerned that the company would die if they didn't change how they did business. With Charles Perry, AUDG president, acting as the cornerstone of the effort, leadership got on their knees and humbled themselves before God. God recognized their faithfulness, humbleness, and obedience and rained blessing down upon them so great that even today they still shake their heads in amazement and say, "Thank You, God."

The group's faith grew as a result of what happened, but that was only the beginning. They shared their faith with the university officials, architects, engineers, contractors, lawyers, and bankers. Only God knows how many lives this affected. It impacted Mike Godwin's life individually and many others with Ambling. God made Himself clearly evident to all who were either involved or simply observing, and that strengthened everyone's faith.

Kevin King, part of the senior leadership team at Ambling, had this to say about the company: "I think as long as we continue to recognize that we are the tools and not the author of any success at Ambling and glorify God by publicly proclaiming His hand in our decisions and acknowledging His blessings, we can retain His anointing. If we take our eyes off Him, that anointing can go as surely as it came."

AUDG president, Charles Perry, said, "God delivers answers to our personnel needs in a way that cannot be denied, ignored, or explained in any other way. When we humble ourselves, openly place God first in our lives and are obedient, then God is extremely abundant in His blessing to us." With leadership like Charles and Kevin, Mike can't help but have a great business.

Since Mike has put God in the center of everything, people have moved from all over the country to Valdosta, Georgia, to work with him. "We'll talk about a specific position that we need to fill and say, 'Well, we'll never get that person in Valdosta,' and then lo and behold! right out of the sky someone will call and say, 'Hey, my wife's getting transferred to Valdosta . . .'" Yes, God does work in mysterious ways!

Mike emphasizes that he recruits some of the finest people in the business based on the candidates' biblical values, stating that every business is founded first and foremost on its mission and values. He believes that people won't follow those they don't trust, so you must have integrity and follow biblical values if you want to lead. He feels the business has thrived, as has his family and community life, because he and his wife demonstrate their beliefs and faith with their actions.

Mike has made more money than he ever dreamed he would make, but he also says with emphasis, "I am not driven by money. I continue to give back. We want to be a company that continually gives back to our church and to our community." With over 85 percent employee involvement, Ambling built a Habitat for Humanity house. Mike said it would have been easy for them to write a fifty-thousand-dollar check for that purpose, but the involvement of his people was infinitely more important, emphasizing again that you teach faithfulness by your actions and by supporting the right things.

Another bottom-line factor is that Mike's wife, Jayne, is a big supporter of Mike and his efforts. She is strong in her Christian faith. He says that without the support of his wife, "I don't know where I would be today." Jayne continually lifts him and the business up in prayer.

Today Mike still relies upon fundamental biblical beliefs and has built his business up to roughly eleven hundred people. He and Jayne continue to be very grateful and understand that these blessings come from God. Mike knows that his time on earth will pass, so if he is to leave a lasting legacy, he needs to do the right thing by sharing his faith with others.

TOM HARKEN

I speak of your faithfulness and salvation.
I do not conceal your love and your truth
from the great assembly.

—PSALM 40:10 NIV

Tom Harken is one of the most remarkable men I've ever met.
The height of his success is even more amazing when you realize the depth of the adversity he overcame.

Tom's first serious job was serving in the United States Air Force.
When his commitment was over, he went to work for the Kirby
Vacuum Cleaner Company and became the top-selling salesman in
the nation. Then he decided to sell recreational vehicles and became
the industry's top-selling independent broker. Tom really hit his stride
when he opened his first Casa Olé restaurant in 1979. Eventually, his
business grew to include over eight hundred employees in thirteen
Casa Olé and Crazy Jose's Mexican restaurants, which he sold in 2004.

The adversity Tom has overcome in his life made him a shoo-in
for the Horatio Alger Award, which he was honored to receive in
1992. He has also been humbled by the number of honorary degrees
bestowed on him from distinguished universities. Tom said it always
amazes him to get one, and he's somewhat fearful that if they find
out he can't spell *honorary,* they might even take it back.

You see, Tom suffered quite a bit of illness when he was a youngster and as a result missed a lot of school and eventually dropped
out. For most of his first thirty years, he was illiterate.

Tom has been helping the battle against illiteracy by giving motivational speeches at universities, Fortune 500 companies, churches,

and schools. But, he says, "Never in my life had I ever experienced the following situation." Tom proceeded to tell me that one day he received a call in his office from a famed university—in fact, one of the oldest in the nation. Some of the most prominent people in the world have been educated there, and they invited Tom to deliver the commencement address that year. He would learn later they were presenting him with an honorary doctorate of commercial science.

According to Tom, the university really rolled out the red carpet for him, and that evening he went to dinner with the provost, deans, faculty, and spouses. During the course of the evening, a dean leaned over and commented, "Mr. Harken, I've read a lot about you and your speeches, and I hope you're not going to bring up much about religion or God. We like to stay neutral." Tom said that while he was absorbing this statement, the dean asked him what his intended subject would be. Tom responded, "Normally I speak about how God helped me, along with my wife, Miss Melba, to overcome enormous odds in my learning disabilities, especially the fact that I couldn't read as an adult." The dean said nothing further, and Tom let it pass with no comment.

But Tom was truly surprised, as until that moment he had never been told what to say or what not to say. Before going to sleep that night, he called his wife and told her what had happened. She asked what he was going to do, and he answered, "I don't really know yet." She responded, "God will tell you what to say."

Attending the big event the next evening were hundreds of students, faculty, visitors, and of course the administration. "We donned our ceremonial caps and gowns and marched in together. With the preliminaries over, they presented me with the honorary degree and then introduced me as speaker." Tom said that much to his surprise, the first words out of his mouth were, "If ever there was a university that needed God, it's this one right here, right now! If you don't know God, you're in trouble. Go find Him." Tom said the audience stood and gave him a thunderous ovation. "I looked behind me to my left and right and could see the educators slowly coming to their feet. I think they had been forced to stand by the audience, and I went on to tell that part of the world we need God in our lives more than ever today, and we also will need Him tomorrow. The remainder of the speech centered on how they also needed a great education and how fortunate everyone was to be there that evening because God had been present every step of the way."

Tom went ahead to say with a wide grin, "After the speech there was another standing ovation. Of course I felt great! Then came the reception. I didn't know what to expect because I'd be mingling with the university VIPs. I was late arriving because I had promised the students a copy of my little laminated verse, 'God's Minute,' in exchange for a hug. This took about an hour. At that reception, much to my surprise, not one derogatory remark was made. Administrators, deans, and faculty, trustees even, all wanted a hug and a 'God's Minute.' Some even hugged me, saying, 'We needed that speech today.'

"Miss Melba was right: God told me what to say. I left that university with my head held high and my heart filled with much joy, knowing that God speaks louder than money. From the letters I received afterward, I know I made a difference."

Tom went on to say that this university accepts money from very prominent people, some of whom are atheists, and this has contributed to turning that university from a historically Christ-centered foundation to a neutral position. "They built a beautiful facility, but on that occasion I went straight to the heart. It's amazing how God can use us sometimes to reach those who need to hear the true Word. Of course, should it ever happen again, wherever I am I will do the same thing, no question about it."

You would really have to know Tom Harken to appreciate the magnitude of what he did and the way he lives his life, how he is always encouraging other people, speaking out concerning his faith and his family, and how great it is to be an American.

I'll say it again, again, and yet again: when we are faithful to honor God, He honors us. When we let our faith shine before men the results are catching, and others join the mighty throng. Countless generations of people will benefit. There is no way to measure what the student body and faculty received as a direct result of the bold and faithful witness of one man who loves his Lord and loves his fellow man, and makes contributions to them on a steady basis.

CHAPTER 8

GENTLENESS

The Lord's bond-servant must not be quarrelsome, but be kind to all, able to teach, patient when wronged, with gentleness correcting those who are in opposition, if perhaps God may grant them repentance leading to the knowledge of the truth, and they may come to their senses and escape from the snare of the devil, having been held captive by him to do his will.

—2 Timothy 2:24–26

The transformed are humble before God and their meekness of heart (the opposite of self-assertive, bold, prideful, or arrogant) is a delight unto Him. Jesus taught gentleness as a virtue. No philosopher through the ages of time taught that meekness or gentleness was a strength. And yet gentleness in a believer's spirit delights God. Our gentleness honors Him. It shows our willing submission to Him without complaint or rebelliousness.

Two entrepreneurial businessmen have stories that reveal their fruit of gentleness: Albert Black, founder of On-Target Supplies & Logistics, and Bob Lightner, founder of Potter's Ranch Wilderness Retreat. If you are one of the many who confuse gentleness with weakness, you won't be confused after you read these two stories. Both of these men are strong because they are meek!

ALBERT BLACK

Who among you is wise and understanding? Let him show by his good behavior his deeds in the gentleness of wisdom.

—James 3:13

Albert Black is a remarkable man with a strong physical presence that commands attention, invites respect, and breeds trust and confidence in his listeners. This is true whether the listener is a member of his staff, in a civic group, or in a one-on-one conversation with him. Few would guess that a man with such an imposing physical presence would be admired most for his meek and gentle spirit.

Albert has a knack for winning friends and influencing people by showing them a better way to do things. He plainly demonstrates that you don't build a business; you build people—and people build the business. It was my privilege to be given a tour of his facility, a former crack house that he converted to a warehouse and headquarters for people who were hungry for leadership and opportunity.

Albert Black's work life began early; he started his first business when he was just eight years old. That first entrepreneurial venture came when he rented a push mower, knocked on doors, and cut yards in the neighborhood.

He points out that his father had worked at a hotel and loved to help people. As the doorman, his father came to know some of Dallas's business leaders. Later on, he inspired Albert to be a business leader.

It was not an easy path he followed. After finishing college and going into business, cash flow was considerably less than needed to survive. Albert and his wife, Gwyneith, each got jobs to support the business. Albert got a second job and worked nights, but he definitely had major objectives in life. He wanted to earn money, but he also wanted to be a student in the process and develop management ability and competency so he could take that into his company and make it work.

Albert founded On-Target Industrial Maintenance & Supply in 1982 and later changed the name to On-Target Supplies & Logistics. The company currently employs approximately 180 people and generates over $40 million in sales. He got his first clients by taking the direct approach—traveling the streets, looking for customers wherever people could be found. His motive, however, was the thing I believe made the difference: Albert went into business to create jobs to hire people. He believes that is God's work, and that's what he wanted to be involved in. He wanted to improve the infrastructure of inner cities, employ people, and let people know he was doing business in the neighborhood.

He built his business with a hands-on approach. He listens, plans, and presents in order to perform, to review, and to adjust to what corporate clients need today. He observes that many companies are proud of the fact that they move things from their dock to the consumer's dock. With his innovation, technology savvy, and heart for the business, along with his marvelous insights, he was able to create a "from our desk to your desk" for the same price, saving money and time and giving his clients something extra.

When it was my privilege to tour his facilities, I was prepared to be impressed because I had talked to his trusted assistant, Georgie Cornelius, and her cheerful, efficient manner was quite extraordinary.

Albert has the ability to evaluate individuals and discern whether or not they should be part of his team. But that's just part of his effectiveness. In response to an employment ad his company placed, an extremely overweight young man waited in the reception area.

When Mr. Black noticed him, he invited him into his office. The young man asked why he had singled him out, and Mr. Black responded he knew that because of his weight the young man would not be hired anywhere else. Albert wanted him to work in his company because he knew the young man had value and believed he could be of help to him. Albert Black's honesty coupled with gentleness has worked out quite well. The young man's gratitude was evident. During the time he worked for Mr. Black, he lost much of the weight and made good progress toward being a more balanced person and a successful employee.

Albert has also been active in his community, working in several capacities at the Greater Dallas Chamber of Commerce, Dallas Black Chamber, and many more organizations. He believes it's good business and good citizenship to demonstrate leadership, so he worked with nonprofit organizations in and around town as a volunteer, which reveals his heart, but he also knew it would give him and his company the type of exposure that would enable them to build a reputation in Dallas.

Albert repeatedly says, "As a business leader, I think what we have to do is learn to listen and learn, teach and preach, coach and counsel." He says, "When we do these things we become effective leaders, and if we don't prepare ourselves for that type of leadership, the organization will grow bigger than us and we'll risk losing our position."

He is a strong believer in education not only for himself but for those he brings aboard. After Albert finished college on a football scholarship, he completed his MBA at Southern Methodist University in 1995. He believes that every business has an obligation to train and educate its people so they can move up the ladder in their careers and be of substantially more value to the organization. One thing he does, which is truly unusual, is strongly encourage his people to get a college education during the daytime and work only part time, so they can be at home with their families at night. He says he has never lost in the long run on anyone with this approach. He has financed many employees' way through college. He doesn't even require that they have a high school diploma before he starts the educational process.

If it were possible for you to go through Albert's On-Target organization and witness the excitement and enthusiasm, the courtesy and respect with which each person is treated, and the relationships he's built with all of them, you would certainly be inspired. He gets involved in their personal lives; he encourages all employees to be part of the On-Target retirement plan, and he wants them to be a "20 percent saver," pointing out that the law permits most people to save as much as 20 percent and his company matches 25 percent. "That's too advantageous for people not to be involved in," Albert says.

He also encourages his employees to use their money wisely. Since he believes everyone should have a financial game plan, he smiles as he says, "We twist a lot of arms to get people involved." That arm twisting has resulted in 95 percent of his employees being enrolled in his company's 401(k) plan.

Not only does he do those things, but perhaps the most unusual business approach he takes occurs every Friday morning at their staff meeting. "All employees get a chance to teach, preach, coach, counsel, listen, and learn from our fellow employees. We get a chance to share the books of the company, the financial statements of the company. This goes beyond just open book managing into actually teaching and receiving feedback from these financials. And all of that goes with a continental breakfast."

Albert follows biblical principles and openly shares about his faith. He wants to do what is right by his employees. He knows that when his employees get an education, not only are they ensuring a better future, but the examples they are setting in the neighborhood will enable their families to also be successful. In short, role models abound in his organization.

Mr. Black promises his people three things. First, he promises them an *educational income*. If you work with Albert Black, you will know how to run a business. On-Target has an open-book accounting system, so employees who decide to start their own business later will know how—they will know every expense in the business, how to manage a revenue stream, how to figure the cost of sales, how to run a business in a couple of years. That's the educational income.

On-Target also pays the employees a *psychological income*. "We want them to feel good about what they're doing at On-Target Supplies & Logistics. This coming in with *esprit de corps*, that attitude that says 'Together we can climb mountains and win battles.' That's what we offer the people."

The last promise and most important for some (but the least important for Albert Black) is the *financial income*. On-Target consistently pays above market. The average income of his employees is $29,800. In his neighborhood, that's quite a sum of money. He says, "We don't want anybody to think that coming to work for On-Target Supplies & Logistics means they have to give up the opportunity to earn maximum salary." Albert clearly understands the purpose of being in business—to create jobs. He knows it's God's work. He has surrounded himself with a wise board of advisors, and he knows that as a service provider people are his only real asset. He believes and teaches that example is the best teacher, and often says, "People would rather see a sermon than hear one." Albert Black's business is a success because he is a success with people. He is a success with people because of his heart for them.

On-Target's employees understand that for all the compassion Albert has, he is running a business and teaching others how to run a business. As he often reminds his people, "Work works." For example, if a person is late to work once, he explains to him or her why being late is unacceptable. He tells them since they are suppliers, if one person is late it slows down the entire operation because the others have to pitch in and do that job. If the employee is late twice, he puts it on the employee's report. The third time that individual is late, he is suspended for two days without pay. The fourth time it happens, Albert permits him to secure employment elsewhere. He points out that just because an organization has a big heart doesn't mean it has a small mind.

He makes it a point to train labor to take a look at the future and embrace it. "We have to make sure they're prepared by making sure that we've saved and invested properly in order to finance the future." And yes, he still harkens back to his parents. He believed his mother was a driver and she expected nothing but the best. "She was an elitist in her own right, and she didn't think that she should expect anything but the best from her children. That drives the way we run On-Target Supplies & Logistics."

He's a stickler for the little things. He says, "We have to speak correctly, walk correctly, have good posture, be clean, make the best grades in school. We have to look at ourselves as champions of whatever cause we are a part of. We lived in the ghetto, but," he says, "my mother wouldn't permit us to think that way. She used to say, 'You may live in the ghetto, but you're not ghetto material and I won't stand for you acting that way.'"

Albert points out, "Whatever character that I may be able to have was formed by my grandmother—to treat people with passion, Christian passion; to always look out, as she would say, for the other fellow; to do what you say you're going to do; to take care of others before you take care of yourself; to tell the truth; to love and expect to be loved; to put God first, your family second, and everything else somewhere after that."

Albert believes that small business owners have to teach and preach, coach and counsel, and truly believe that people are good, that people have potential, that people want to learn and grow like he has done. "You should learn to grow the people who've joined you on your path. Those people will grow the business."

How true! And what a marvelous lesson in this story that all of us can benefit enormously by emulating.

BOB LIGHTNER

But flee from these things, you man of God, and pursue righteousness, godliness, faith, love, perseverance and gentleness.

—1 TIMOTHY 6:11

Robert J. (Bob) Lightner was born in 1946, long before the word *dysfunctional* was applied to families like his. After his parents divorced, Bob began to think he had to fight his way through life to survive. He and his four brothers grew up on the streets and boasted that they could finish most fights, regardless of who started them. Fortunately, Bob's rough and rocky start in life did not keep him from becoming the gentle man God intended him to be.

Today Bob Lightner chooses to define his life not by his accomplishments, but by the moments and choices that changed its direction. His first defining moment came on April 30, 1965, when he married Jeanette Berry. Frail and beautiful, Jeanette took over his heart from the moment he first saw her. She was the love of his life. They started their marriage on a shoestring while Bob worked numerous jobs—stock boy, short-order cook, store clerk, groundskeeper at a golf course, truck driver, and factory worker, to name a few.

So how did a man like Bob Lightner move forward to found a travel agency, a bank, an insurance agency, and build the marvelous Potter's Ranch Wilderness Retreat?

One of Bob's defining moments was becoming a father. Bob and Jeannette had three sons: Brian, Tom, and Wesley. After Brian arrived, the magnitude of the responsibility of fatherhood raised lots of questions and created a feeling of unrest in Bob. Tom's birth accentuated Bob's unrest, and on January 26, 1973, after much prayer by his friends and wife, Bob received Christ into his heart when he heard three laymen share their testimony of how Christ had changed their lives.

When Bob Lightner committed his life to Christ, he started seeking Christ's will in everything he did. Prayer and Bible study became a vital part of Bob's daily life. Because he put Christ at the center of his life, Bob also put Christ at the center of his marriage. He openly discussed the Bible, church, work, and family matters with his family and quit work early on Fridays to spend special "date" time with Jeanette.

The Lightners are a classic example of a husband and wife who follow biblical principles, have a happy family life, and enjoy financial security while also contributing much to their community. They used biblical principles in parenting and in running their business. They taught their children the biblical principles of loving others, working for God, using their God-given gifts for His glory, and giving more than one might ask or expect. They believe in going the extra mile and not yielding or compromising their principles for anyone. They set aside family time when the children were young, and though their sons have long been grown, they still get together twice a week as family.

With a clearer, Christ-based focus, Bob was able to push aside his desire to settle things through physical or mental power struggles and take a gentler approach to problems. He realized that God was leading him to greater things when a factory accident convinced him that through God he could do anything if he only believed and followed His will for his life (Philippians 4:13).

It was a huge leap of faith that led Bob into the insurance business when he was twenty-nine years old. With a limited high school education, his friends advised him against the move, but Bob felt strongly that this was what God wanted him to do. As it turned out, each step he took in this new business afforded him an opportunity to share his faith with his clients, and he's done that ever since. Later, as he trained his agents in the industry, he had an opportunity to share his faith with them. And as the owner and developer of his own agency, through work principles, company mission statements, and daily procedures that glorified God, Bob's agents were each able to seek God's will.

Today Bob knows the definition of true success. He is grateful to be the spiritual leader in a home where every family member has come to know the love of God, their Creator. Now Bob is sixty years into this journey, but he has realized that with each passing day God has been in control and, "I've had a wonderful ride!" Now he has ample time to consider all the things that God has blessed him with, including church, family, and actively participating in Potter's Ranch, the Christian wilderness retreat center that God allowed him to develop.

Bob asks, "What do I do next? God only knows. I wake up excited every morning, singing His praises as I await His leadership into the next adventure. With a wonderful wife, three great sons, three beautiful daughters-in-law, and ten lovely grandchildren, I praise God for His richest blessings, only awaiting that moment when He will say to me, 'Well done, good and faithful servant. Come and share your Master's happiness.'"

I've known Bob and his family for many years, and I've seen him in many different situations. His upbeat, loving, and gentle spirit is always visible. He never hesitates to give God the credit for all the blessings that have come his way. He looks forward to every tomorrow in his life and is ready to go when the Lord decides that his venue on earth has been upgraded. He knows he will get to spend eternity with His Lord and Savior.

It's safe to say that Robert J. Lightner will testify—and he does often—that God's way is not only the best way, but the *only* way to reap those beautiful benefits here on earth that come with peace of mind and the assurance that your eternity is secure.

Bob Lightner has impacted the lives of many because he listens to God, listens to counsel, searches the Scriptures, and bathes everything in prayer. He encourages those he works with and loves to follow the same procedure.

Following are Bob's favorite Bible verses and how he applies them to his life.

"But if any of you lacks wisdom, let him ask of God, who gives to all generously and without reproach, and it will be given to him"(James 1:5). Bob says, "I have used this verse on everything in my Christian life. I seek wisdom and teach others as well to slow down and do the same, pray on it, sleep on it over one or more nights. God knows it doesn't matter if it's a minor or major thing that I do. I ask God to help me, to show me, to direct me or to stop me. Whatever He knows is best for my life. Give me wisdom to know."

"The thief comes only to steal and kill and destroy; I came that they may have life, and have it abundantly" (John 10:10). About this verse, Bob says, "I speak a lot to people about this scripture when I am ministering to, encouraging, or helping direct someone when they are open for that. The full life is Christ living in us, and everything else is an additional bonus He allows in our life."

"A good name is to be more desired than great wealth, favor is better than silver and gold" (Proverbs 22:1). Bob says, "I have shared with everyone in my businesses over the years and many boards that I have served on that your name is given one time to your life . . . *it is you*! What is it worth or what would it take to destroy who you are? God has made you special, so build your name to mean something where you live and work. Do it every day! It is worth far more than any money you might acquire."

Yes, Bob Lightner's early life was full of street fights, but the transforming love of Christ changed him into a man who prayerfully and gently leads people to know Jesus Christ and to seek the wisdom of the Lord.

CHAPTER 9

SELF-CONTROL

*I have been crucified with Christ; and it is no longer I
who live, but Christ lives in me; and the life which I now
live in the flesh I live by faith in the Son of God, who
loved me and gave Himself up for me.*

—GALATIANS 2:20

Transformed Christians seek to practice self-control and to be
obedient to the Word because of the love they have for God.
They pray for the ability to control themselves and adhere to Scripture, which admonishes them to take even their thoughts captive.
Through the Holy Spirit, we are given the fruit of self-control and
that which we cannot do by our own power is done for us.

In their early lives, self-control was hard to come by for businessman and evangelist Dave Curry, retired businessman and state senator Bill Costas, and neurosurgeon Dr. Ben Carson, but the love of
the Lord made it not only possible, but a constant part of their lives.

Dave Curry

Do you not know that those who run in a race all run,
but only one receives the prize? Run in such a way that
you may win. Everyone who competes in the games
exercises self-control in all things.

—1 Corinthians 9:24–25

Dave Curry shares his testimony with thousands of people every year. Yet he is an unlikely evangelist because, when he was a child, his mother told him that when he did anything wrong God would punish him, that he would never amount to anything, and that he was destined to be just like her alcoholic father.

Because of his mother's own tough childhood and poor self-image, when Dave's mother looked at him she saw everything her alcoholic father represented and when she looked at Dave's sister, she saw everything she always wanted to be. She was very obvious about who her favorite child was—and it sure wasn't Dave.

Dave's parents fought violently throughout his childhood, and he was so afraid he frequently ran away from home. An uncle who was a professional gambler taught him how to hustle pool and play cards so he could make some money. By age fifteen, Dave was a compulsive gambler.

Two days before Dave's seventeenth birthday, tragedy struck the family. Dave's sister, a Christian whom his mother adored, developed a brain tumor and after seven surgeries died at age twenty-one. Two weeks later, after a heated argument, his mother asked, "Why couldn't it have been you? She was my whole life, and you will amount to nothing." His mother informed him that God was going to punish him for his lifestyle. Dave's response was to run from God for nine years after his sister's death, looking for peace.

It is easy to understand why Dave's self-image was so poor. Even his schoolteachers told him he'd amount to nothing, and his school records indicated they were probably right. He graduated at the bottom of his class. He married his wife one week out of high school, but he continued gambling. He had promised his sister before she died that one day he would commit his life to Christ, which he did in 1969. Then came the first glimmer of hope. Dave says the Lord took his gambling habit away immediately and he's never gambled since.

In 1970, Dave started a heating and air conditioning business with five employees. By 1979, the company had expanded to six locations. Yet due to a bad economy and some unwise decisions, he lost millions of dollars in assets in ninety days and was forced into bankruptcy. The IRS assessed him thousands of dollars in back taxes. He opened two restaurants in Dallas in 1984 and was broke again in 1985. Dave understands that failure is an event, but at that point in his life it appeared it was going to be a habit.

After the restaurants failed, Dave came to work for our company, the Zig Ziglar Corporation. Today he tells his audiences that the years he worked at Ziglar were his best because he finally learned to like himself. In 1992, Dave moved to Boulder, Colorado, to work for a major company. Sixty days after he arrived to fill his executive position, he and every other executive were fired when a bank took over the management of the company. There seemed to be no end to his business failures, but the good news is a lot of business people in his audiences relate to those failures very well. He shares that he wanted to return to Dallas, but that God made it clear he was to stay. For the first time in eighteen years, Dave says, he listened to God and stayed in Boulder.

Dave purchased a Crestcom Training franchise in 1993 and says the Lord has blessed his business. Dave gives glory to God for taking all of his failures and turning them into outstanding successes. He shares the Bible verses that he clung to, telling how he has lived out Romans 8:28 in both his business and family life. He explains that Philippians 4:13 reminded him that without the strength of Christ he could do nothing. Proverbs 3:5–6 has been his guide for doing business, and 1 John 5:13 gives him the assurance of eternal life. Dave travels all over the country at his own expense to share his testimony, and over the years hundreds have come to know Christ because of Dave's commitment.

Dave shares that his beautiful wife has always been his biggest cheerleader. He tells the audiences that as a Christian in a legalist environment he had become as narrow minded as Archie Bunker. As a result, there were three things he said he would not tolerate as the father of his three children. One was divorce—because his parents divorced after thirty-eight years of marriage and it devastated the family. Second was drugs—because he had no use for people who used drugs. Third was that his children could not date people from other races—because that is what he had been taught growing up.

He tells his audiences that his older daughter married a much older man while she was in law school, and two years later went through a tough divorce. Dave's son became a drug addict in his early twenties, and he shares the hurt the family went through in that situation, but also how God delivered his son from his addiction. He talks about how his youngest daughter became pregnant by an African-American boy, and Dave became furious. He remembered reading about the same circumstances in Bill McCartney's book *Ashes to Glory*, so he called Bill, who was head coach at Colorado University in Boulder at that time. He met with Bill once a week for several weeks as they worked through the process. But then came a moment of epiphany one morning while he was shaving. Looking at himself in the mirror, he saw his mother had been right. But God reminded him of Revelation 3:17 and impressed this upon Dave's heart, *We are all born poor, blind, wretched, and naked. Dave Curry, when you came to Me, I accepted you that way—unconditionally, with no strings attached. When this baby comes into the world, he will be poor, blind, and naked. It is not his fault, and you need to accept him unconditionally, with no strings attached.*

Dave recalls that at that moment, a peace came over him like he had never felt since his salvation. He now proudly says, "The greatest thing that has happened to me other than my wife and salvation is my biracial grandson, Braxton." He says Braxton taught him to love as Jesus loved—unconditionally, with no strings attached. He also shares that his daughter has since married an outstanding Christian man who loves her and has adopted Braxton.

If God can take Dave Curry and all of his difficulties and hang-ups and use him as a mighty warrior for the kingdom, he can use you too. Much of Dave's early training was not according to biblical principles, but Dave was willing to change and grow as God guided him, and the Lord blessed him in ways he could never have imagined.

Dave made it clear that his self-control comes from the Lord when he said the Lord removed his addiction to gambling. The Lord showed him how the things he had prideful arrogance about could happen even in his family, and the Lord gave Dave the unconditional love he needed to have for his biracial grandson, Braxton.

Some people get indirect lessons from the Lord and some get very direct lessons. If I didn't know better, I'd say that Dave Curry had his lessons delivered straight to the heart! Fortunately, he was able to withstand all the pruning and he is a better man for all his trials. Dave's story reminds us that with the goal of becoming more like Jesus ever before us, joy, love, and acceptance will abound.

BILL COSTAS

We are taking every thought captive to the obedience of Christ.

—2 CORINTHIANS 10:5

It's true—Bill Costas has "been there and done that." Like all of us, he has experienced several setbacks and detours along his life's journey, but through the grace of God and the discipline of self-control, he is now thriving and making a positive impact on those around him.

The son of immigrants from Greece, Bill Costas has done many things, from running a supermarket to serving as state senator of Indiana for two four-year terms. He has learned the lessons of hard work and the importance of being a servant. As you will see, many of his learning experiences were particularly painful, and most of them had to do with lack of self-control!

Though he had a big church wedding, Bill saw no need to attend church on a regular basis. That might help explain some of the choices he later made. After the wedding, Bill worked for his father-in-law in the wholesale produce business. He and his bride started having problems almost immediately but Bill took the easy route, refusing to argue and instead withdrawing from the relationship. He and his wife eventually had three lovely children, but their relationship stayed at a surface level.

About the same time the wholesale produce business started to slow down, supermarkets were becoming popular. Bill and a partner opened Wilco Foods, but they went separate ways because their personalities clashed. Bill took on two new partners, including his father-in-law, and the store experienced huge success.

Bill is outgoing and likeable, but a touch of wanderlust led him to some very difficult times. He was living on the wild side, so his father-in-law and partner asked him to get control of himself. When he didn't, they had to fire him—and they had to make sure he would get the message. So one day the sheriff came to Bill's office with a court order that said he had to vacate the premises within four hours. Because of Bill's indiscretions, his wife divorced him. He went on unemployment and received forty-nine dollars a week—quite a drop from the thousand-dollar-a-week paycheck he had been earning.

Difficulties arose in negotiating the sale of his business. During this time, Bill recognized that he needed God to help him straighten out his life. He remembered that his mother had always told him that Jesus loved him, and he became a believer.

After his commitment to Christ, Bill started reading the Bible and abandoned his friends who were short of character. He also had a girlfriend, but in studying God's Word he came to understand that sex outside of marriage is wrong and he ended that relationship as well. In God's Word, he learned he needed to be fair, honest, and morally clean, all of which took self-control, and these realizations changed his life.

God gave Bill a new respect for women, and he asked God for forgiveness for the lifestyle he had lived. He attended a weeklong Christian character-building seminar that strengthened his faith, and he started trusting God for everything.

Like many of us, Bill had his ups and downs, going from having an abundance of money to being close to bankruptcy. When his business partners finally settled with him, he built his store and opened Costas Foods in 1972. The first six months were miserable. He was losing money and wanted to sell but couldn't find a buyer. As he prayed, he felt encouraged, and after the first year the business became profitable.

Difficult times, yes, but Bill had promised the Lord he would always open the store with prayer in the morning and he wouldn't open on Sunday, and he didn't, even though the bank was pressuring him to do so. It appears God had His hand on him because he avoided disaster.

He started having weekly meetings with his managers for prayer and Bible study. He spoke regularly about his faith, making it a point to take about ten minutes during new employee training to give his testimony, explain why the Bible was so important to him, and present each new employee with a Bible. They weren't required to take the Bible, but Bill had signed it with the employee's name. During the thirty years he owned the business, just about everyone accepted the Bible. Bill is proud because he ran his business as God would have him run it, and that meant treating not only his customers fairly but his employees as well.

When his sons graduated from college, Bill invited them to join him in the store. Soon they opened another store, and then another. At one time they employed 325 people.

There was an interesting turn of events when Bill had to replace his bookkeeper because she was expecting a baby. Diane applied for a job at the store because she had heard Bill was a Christian. She had been raised in a Mennonite home and had been married, but her husband was a womanizer. After forgiving him several times, when she was pregnant with her third daughter she couldn't take his indiscretions any longer and divorce followed. Not long after Diane began working for the store, Bill started taking an interest in her. She had been praying for a godly man, and Bill had been praying for a godly woman. As they shared Christ at work their relationship grew, and finally they decided, almost impetuously, that they would marry almost immediately.

Bill did the old-fashioned thing by going to Diane's dad and asking permission to marry his daughter. Her father wondered why they were in such a big hurry, but Bill was pleasantly insistent and the wedding was arranged. What followed was a helter-skelter, pandemonium-laced few days as they got everything together. This brought the two families together, and they daily got on their knees and asked God's blessings.

Their family blended Bill's daughter and two sons with Diane's three girls, Whitney, Marcy, and Jamie, whom he later adopted. The large family soon learned to live together well and are now very close and experiencing the blessings of God.

In 1975 Bill ran for the US Senate, and in 1976 and 1978 he ran for Congress. In 1980 he was elected to the Indiana State Senate, an office he held for eight years. That same year at the requests of his sons, he opened an auto service center in the adjoining property at the supermarket, and later opened two additional supermarkets and a car wash. Then, in 1998, Bill sold the store at a good profit.

After selling the store, Bill and Diane decided to take a trip to Israel. At the required physical, the doctors discovered a spot on Bill's lung. They went to the Mayo Clinic and learned the spot on his lung was cancerous. Treatment followed and today he is cancer free. The Lord has also seen Bill through a potentially fatal heart surgery. These experiences have strengthened Bill's fervent desire to share his faith.

Yes, Bill has matured in his faith, and self-control is now the rule of the day. Over the years he built a great reputation. When he decided to run for the US Senate, he easily collected signatures from eleven congressional districts. Because of his reputation, he was invited to participate in a debate with the other candidates. Since his last name starts with "C" he spoke before the other candidates, Lugar (former mayor of Indianapolis) and Whitcomb (former governor of Indiana). In the debate Bill was quite bold in speaking about his Christian faith. This set the tone for the debate, and the other two candidates put their written speeches aside and spoke from the heart as well.

Bill, now age seventy-six, asked God to not cast him off at the time of old age and "do not forsake me when my strength fails" (Psalm 71:9). His life has been a series of exciting adventures. He's had his ups and downs, but because he trusts God and is obedient to Him and shares his faith wherever he goes, the day will come when he will be lifted up. Bill is excited about his faith and his eternal future.

Bill's story should be an object lesson for all of us that when we put our faith in Christ, the eventual result is eternity with Him and with those we've loved here on earth who know Christ as Lord. It's true—God's way is still the best way.

DR. BEN CARSON

He who is slow to anger is better than the mighty,
And he who rules his spirit, than he who captures a city.
—PROVERBS 16:32

Many people say that Dr. Ben Carson, director of pediatric neurosurgery and professor of neurological surgery at Johns Hopkins Hospital, is brilliant. He smilingly says, "Yes, they give me a lot of credit, but the reality is any innovative or creative ideas I brought to the profession, particularly as it relates to conjoined twins, is simply a gift from God." He makes it clear that God gives him direction and ideas.

Dr. Carson, a winner of the prestigious Horatio Alger Award, is internationally recognized and respected today, but his story could have turned out much differently. At age fourteen, he attempted to stab another youngster with a large camping knife. The blade struck a metal buckle under the young man's clothing and broke, leaving him unharmed.

Ben was horrified when he realized that he was so out of control he had tried to kill someone over a meaningless incident. He locked himself in the bathroom and poured his heart out to God. He said, "As I contemplated the horrors awaiting me because of my temper, I picked up the Bible and began reading verses from the book of Proverbs." There were many verses that dealt with anger and the trouble it gets you into, but the one that really impressed him was Proverbs 16:32: "He who is slow to anger is better than the mighty, and he who rules his spirit, than he who captures a city."

Ben spent three hours contemplating, praying, and reading, and he said that when he emerged from the room, he was truly a changed individual. No surprise in that. When we deal directly with our Lord and humble ourselves before Him, He always responds. I wonder, was it really a coincidence that the knife hit the metal belt buckle? We'll never know for sure, but Ben Carson's future was completely altered by the incident. As he says, "That's the day I truly became a Christian." I say, that is the day he also acquired the fruit of self-control.

One of the beautiful things about knowing where you will spend your eternity is the sense of peace and confidence it gives you. Dr. Carson feels that he is privileged to be able to perform surgery that is truly life changing. Neurosurgery is one of the most stressful careers in the world, yet Dr. Carson feels complete peace with what he is doing. He says, "I know that God is in charge and my only responsibility is to do my best and let God do the rest."

One of Dr. Carson's favorite Bible verses is Proverbs 3:5–6, which says, "Trust in the LORD with all your heart and do not lean on your own understanding. In all your ways acknowledge Him, and He will make your paths straight." Dr. Carson quotes this verse to make clear that his source of strength and accomplishment is the Lord. He always seeks the Lord's guidance and wisdom, and he gives God credit for the many seemingly impossible things he has achieved.

When faced with insurmountable obstacles and discouragement, Dr. Carson says Philippians 4:13—"I can do all things through Him who strengthens me"—rejuvenates his enthusiasm and gives him confidence to strive for things others may think impossible.

Dr. Carson is absolutely correct in his understanding that when he does his best, he can relax. God is in control, and we are only responsible to be accountable to Him. We are not responsible for the results, nor can we claim credit for those results.

We cannot claim credit for the love, joy, peace, patience, kindness, goodness, faithfulness, gentleness, and self-control we possess, but we bring honor and glory to God when these fruits of the Holy Spirit are manifested in our lives.

PART FOUR

YOU WILL KNOW THEM *by* THEIR FRUIT

CHAPTER 10

AN INTIMATE RELATIONSHIP

My Father is glorified by this, that you bear much fruit, and so prove to be My disciples. Just as the Father has loved Me, I have also loved you; abide in My love. If you keep My commandments, you will abide in My love; just as I have kept My Father's commandments and abide in His love. These things I have spoken to you so that My joy may be in you, and that your joy may be made full.

—JOHN 15:8–11

The next and final story of a transformed life that is lived with great joy in obedience and availability to the Lord Jesus Christ is a story I am intimately familiar with. The transformation of this individual from totally lost to completely loved and forgiven was so visually apparent that it was astounding, even miraculous, to everyone who was blessed to witness it firsthand.

I had the privilege of baptizing my granddaughter Amey, whom I call "Sunshine," when she was twelve years old, but she was not saved. She did not know Christ as Lord. She got involved in everything that young girls are not supposed to get involved in and ultimately she realized how truly miserable she was.

It is my hope that as you read her story, you will feel the power of the love of Christ in the words I know she prayerfully wrote and that you will see how her personal relationship with Christ makes taking the news of His love into the marketplaces of her life the utmost desire of her heart.

Amey "Sunshine" Fair

He brought me up out of the pit of destruction, out of
the miry clay,
And He set my feet upon a rock making my footsteps firm.
He put a new song in my mouth, a song of praise to our
God;
Many will see and fear, and will trust in the LORD.

—PSALM 40:2–3

I'm really only ten years old. You wouldn't know it to look at me. From the outside, I look like a young woman new to her thirties, but my heart came alive on a warm September night in 1997 when I surrendered my life to God. It was a long twenty-one years leading up to that night.

As a child, I easily accepted that there was a God and frequently spoke to Him. There were believers in my family, but my mom and my stepfather, who professed Christianity, were practicing alcoholics. Consequently, I grew up in a home that practiced a "form of godliness but denied its power" (2 Timothy 3:5).

As I reflect on those years, I can see that the childlike faith I once had began to erode during this time. I felt unsafe and sad and alone as a child. My parents divorced while I was still an infant, and when I was six years old my mother married the man I now refer to as Dad.

I have fond memories of the years my mom and I spent together, just the two of us. I soaked up her attention and even went to work with her sometimes. It never occurred to me that she might be interested in getting married, but when she did I was excited about my new brother and two new sisters. I had a dreamy picture of what life would be like with siblings, so you can imagine my dismay when things didn't go as planned. As anyone who has ever struggled to blend a family knows, it is often a painful and trying adjustment. The next few years were a blur of angry words and fights and abusive situations as my parents struggled with their drinking and each of us tried to figure out our places in the new family.

When I was almost nine years old, my mom came to me one night and told me that she was going to a meeting for people who live with alcoholics. She told me that Dad's drinking had gotten out of hand and she wanted him to get help. After realizing through Al-Anon that she was an alcoholic herself, the two of them began attending meetings together. The next years of my life were spent running around with the other "AA kids" at the meetings. Sometimes it seemed like we lived there, they went so often. It was during this time that my parents began to really discover and depend on God. I saw the transformation taking place and our family began to settle down some, but insecurity had already taken root in my life and the teenage years were just around the corner.

At fourteen I smoked my first cigarette and graduated from there to marijuana and LSD. I got in with a rough crowd in high school and was moved to two more high schools before attending the one I would graduate from. My parents were doing their best to get me into a good school district so that I would hopefully find good friends and start making good choices. It was a geographical cure for a spiritual problem.

We moved to Southlake, Texas, and shortly after I started attending high school I began drinking. Alcohol made me feel bold and funny and uninhibited, and the insecurity seemed to melt away. My self-worth came from my relationships with boys. I made the most awful decisions of my life during the next few years, and ten years later God is still healing me from that time. My drinking eventually landed me in AA, but the temptation of alcohol was too strong to withstand without a real relationship with God.

One thing I have learned since becoming a Christian is that we were created to worship, so if we are not worshiping God, we will find something else to worship. For me, that something else was a boy I met the summer after high school graduation. I spent the next year building my life around him, and the following summer I moved ten hours away from home to be near him where he went to college.

My drinking was at its worst, and though I had quit for a time, I started using drugs again. When the relationship fell apart, I hit a new low. I remember driving back to Dallas in my little red Honda and feeling like I didn't want to live anymore.

The next six months I was so depressed that I often couldn't sleep. At night I would sit on the front porch while the neighborhood slept, trying to devise a new plan for my life that would make everything better. One night I shared my troubles with Mom. She started talking to me about God and inwardly I rolled my eyes. I had heard it all before. She encouraged me to ask God to give me a desire for Him. When my head hit the pillow that night, I muttered a halfhearted prayer to God and drifted off to sleep.

Six months later, God answered that prayer. The ex-boyfriend came into town and we spent the weekend together. His parents told him they would pay for his plane ticket if we would agree to attend church with them on Sunday.

I sat through the evening service on the edge of my seat, not because I was interested in what the speaker was saying, but because I was ready to bolt from that sanctuary! People were raising their hands and crying during the music. I had never seen that before, and I was sure it was unbiblical. Then the tears came without permission, and I felt like I was going to explode. I had to get out of there. I jumped out of my seat and headed for the parking lot.

I couldn't stop crying and I was about as angry as I'd ever been. I couldn't explain the hurricane in my heart. A few minutes later we left and I dropped the ex-boyfriend off at his house. I drove home in tears, full of confusion. I couldn't make sense of my emotions and wrote it off as a bout of hormones. That night I climbed into bed a dead girl. And then God showed up.

There will never be words fit to describe what happened in my bedroom that night. It was a holy visitation. The spirit of the living God descended upon that room and burst into my heart with an all-consuming love. I felt cradled by the hand of God, and as I wept I remember saying, "I give up, I don't know how to live" over and over.

At that moment the Holy Spirit came to live in me, and I saw God for who He was. He was not a Christian way of life. He was not a set of rules. He was not Baptist or Catholic or Presbyterian. He was I AM. He was supernatural and powerful and He was Love—pure, undefiled Love. And for the first time in my life I was clean and totally accepted and wholly loved. I was alive. It must have been two in the morning and I wanted to call my grandparents and tell them I had met God. I was filled with joy, I was overflowing and couldn't sleep for all the excitement. I arose the next morning and started my journey with God.

I found a home church soon after I was born again and was there for about a year when a missionary from Youth with a Mission spoke one Sunday morning. I had been praying, asking God for His plan for my life and when this man began to speak about the mission field my heart leapt up inside me in a way I had never before experienced. I knew that I was called to missions.

I signed up to attend YWAM's training schools and spent the next year of my life on the beautiful campus of YWAM Tyler in

East Texas. God gave me the scripture Hosea 2:14 at that time. It says, "Therefore, behold, I will draw her into the wilderness and speak comfort to her." I grew by leaps and bounds during that year. The Lord had brought me out of the world for a season so that I could be discipled and grow in my relationship with Him, free from temptation and outside distractions.

It was during this year that God delivered me from alcohol addiction and began to heal the wounds I still carried from childhood. It was also during this time that I met Nathan Fair, the man who would become my husband.

That was nine years ago, and I am in awe of this incredible adventure called "relationship with God." I have seen Him use my life to save and to heal. Through Him I have taken the gospel to China, Mongolia, Denmark, Sweden, France, Mexico, Guatemala, and across the United States of America. My husband and I have been blessed with two healthy and beautiful boys, a third child on the way, and a wonderful marriage. As I write this, I can hardly believe it is my own story.

How can I express my gratitude to You, Lord? You are good beyond measure.

With God's Son shining on and in her, Amey truly became my Sunshine girl. Yes, my granddaughter abides in Him and His words abide in her. That she is His disciple is without question for she bears much fruit. Thus God is glorified and as He promised, His joy is in her and her joy has been made full. Praise God!

Amey's transformation, which literally left her glowing, inspired me to seek an even deeper relationship with Jesus Christ than I had previously thought possible—and I found what I was seeking. Most Christians I know have not had the kind of heavenly experience Amey had, but their journey from nonbeliever to ardent follower of Jesus Christ has been every bit as transforming.

Is Something Bothering You?

Have you read these stories and thought, *I'm not like that. I could never be that way, do that thing, feel that way.* Have you considered yourself a Christian, yet you don't see the fruit of the Spirit in your life? Is the transformation missing in your life?

In the introduction of this book, I commented that some Christians don't act like Christians and I believe I know why. They either don't know they don't know Christ or they don't know His Word well enough to know how He wants them to live. Many aren't transformed because they made a decision for Christ with their head instead of with their heart. Maybe they did what Sunshine did when she was twelve years old and got baptized to please their parents. Maybe they decided they believed in God so they walked down the aisle of the church and filled out a card, but they didn't repent of their sins and ask Christ to be the Lord of their life. They didn't lay down their rights to their old sin life and never felt compelled to devour the Word of God. Maybe they didn't experience the remorse one feels for breaking God's heart, nor did they experience the cleansing and renewal that come with God's forgiveness. They just started going to church regularly and began to wonder why they weren't happier, why they didn't feel the joy and peace they saw in other Christians, and they began to think Jesus wasn't as wonderful as they'd been told.

Does that describe you? If so, you are not alone. Not by a long shot! Let me explain. The Barna Research Group of Ventura, California, has discovered that fewer than one out of three people who claim to be born-again Christians adopt the notion of absolute moral truth, that some things are absolutely right and some are absolutely wrong under any and all circumstances, and few Americans turn to their faith as the primary guide for their moral and ethical decisions.

In addition, the Barna study discovered that a substantial number of people who say they are Christians believe that activities such as abortion, gay sex, cohabitation, drunkenness, and viewing pornography are morally acceptable.[1] The Bible clearly states all of these things are wrong and hurtful, yet a worldly attitude persists that anything is okay as long as it doesn't hurt someone else.

The moral principles in the Bible are meant to be the basis of our thoughts and actions, regardless of our preferences, feelings, or situation. We have to learn and grow in our knowledge of Christ and His Word in order to know what the Bible says our moral principles should be. I'm sad to say that many Christians are not discipled or mentored. Consequently, their lives look no different from non-Christians. Ask yourself if your life reflects the life of Christ inside of you.

In this book so far, I have written about God's way being the best way and spreading the good news about Jesus in the marketplace. I've written about transformed Christians and I've shared story after story of individuals whose lives display the obvious fruits of the Spirit and a life lived with biblical wisdom. But nothing I've written thus far is as important as what I'm about to say.

If you haven't already done so, do as my granddaughter Amey did, give up your rebellion against God. Confess that you don't know how to live. Ask Him to be Lord of your life, to bring you up out of the pit of destruction, out of the miry clay. Let Him set your feet upon a rock so that your footsteps will be firm. Invite Him to put a new song in your mouth, a song of praise to Him, so that many in the marketplace of your everyday life will see and fear, and will trust in the Lord.

CHAPTER 11

SHARING CHRIST WITH OTHERS

And Jesus came up and spoke to them, saying,
"All authority has been given to Me in heaven and on
*   earth.*
Go therefore and make disciples of all the nations,
baptizing them in the name of the Father and the Son
*   and the Holy Spirit,*
teaching them to observe all that I commanded you;
and lo, I am with you always, even to the end of the age."
—MATTHEW 28:18–20

Each of the men and women whose stories you have read in this book enjoyed a deep, personal relationship with Jesus Christ that is recognizable to nonbelievers. From Truett Cathy of Chick-fil-A showing the love of Christ to homeless children to Dr. Ben Carson gaining self-control and giving God the credit for his miraculous surgical skills, the people whose fruits of the Spirit we've examined in this book are inspiring examples of how we can take the love of God into the marketplaces of America.

Yet without an abiding relationship with Jesus through which our hearts are filled to overflowing with our praise and devotion to Him, we don't have anything at all to take into the marketplace.

Without that intimate relationship, our attempts to show Jesus to others become a personal effort that does not have the power or direction of the Lord. That kind of fruitless effort is called "works" in Christian circles. Works are akin to spinning your tires when you get your vehicle stuck in the sand. Pressing your accelerator as hard as you can to the floorboard creates a lot of noise and friction, but it doesn't get any results.

Charles Spurgeon once said, "If you have not the Spirit of God, Christian worker, remember that you stand in somebody else's way; you are a fruitless tree standing where a fruitful tree might grow."[1] To effectively take Jesus Christ into your marketplace and share the hope of His love and His glory with others, you must be a transformed Christian, willing to deny self in order to obediently serve Him. All the good works in the world will never attract others to Christ if the person doing the work does not have an intimate, personal relationship with Jesus Christ.

God's goal has never been to simply provide a "fire insurance policy" to keep us out of hell. It has always been to restore us to relationship with Him and get us to a place where we are available so that He can bring glory and honor to Himself through us.

In John 15:7–11, Jesus reveals what is in store for those who abide in Him: "If you abide in Me, and My words abide in you, ask whatever you wish, and it will be done for you. My Father is glorified by this, that you bear much fruit, and so prove to be My disciples. Just as the Father has loved Me, I have also loved you; abide in My love. If you keep My commandments, you will abide in My love; just as I have kept My Father's commandments and abide in His love. These things I have spoken to you so that My joy may be in you, and that your joy may be made full."

The longer we serve God, the better we get to know Him and the more like Jesus we become, thus providing visible proof of the invisible so that the world around us can begin to see the Lord God.

WHY SHOULD WE SHARE
OUR FAITH?

There are many reasons we should share our faith in Christ with others. First, it was the last thing our Lord told us in the Great Commission. Just before He ascended to join His Father in heaven, Jesus said, "All authority has been given to Me in heaven and on earth. Go therefore and make disciples of all the nations, baptizing them in the name of the Father and the Son and the Holy Spirit, teaching them to observe all that I commanded you; and lo, I am with you always, even to the end of the age" (Matthew 28:18–20).

Another reason we should share, or "confess" our experiences with Christ to others is so we are able to experience the blessing of God, as Jesus promised in Luke 12:8–9: "Everyone who confesses Me before men, the Son of Man will confess him also before the angels of God; but he who denies Me before men will be denied before the angels of God."

The reality is if Christ were with you physically, you would be thrilled beyond belief to introduce Him to everyone. Let me remind you that He is alive, and if you are a Christian, He is in you and your very life should reflect His presence. He wants you to tell others about your relationship with Him.

If we intend to do as God has instructed and spread the good news of Jesus Christ, we have to get over the bill of goods we've been sold that we shouldn't impose our religious views on others. I suspect that that conditioning is largely responsible for the awkwardness many feel when they contemplate bringing up their faith. The love of Christ cast wide over the waters of everyday living will bring forth a catch of unexpected proportions. But you can't proclaim the love of Christ just by hoping that you look like a Christian or that people will ask you about Jesus so you won't offend them by telling them about Him without their express permission. Finding ways to create opportunities for discussing Jesus and what He has meant in your life is a logical step toward overcoming that awkwardness.

This chapter is designed to do just that!

PRACTICAL WAYS TO SHARE CHRIST

As we consider how we can share Christ with others in our everyday lives, we should start with prayer. I believe Christians should always pray about what we say and how we are to give an effective witness to others so that we don't rush in with our own ideas, insensitive to what the Lord would have us do. We need to remember that we are not the cause of the effect when we witness and share Jesus. He is the cause and if we allow Him, we can and will be used by Him. He calls on us to tell others about Him, but the end result of our telling is all up to Him.

So, as you prayerfully submit your life and your days to the Lord's leading, here are some simple, practical ways you can share your faith in Christ with others.

Fish and Seven Pin

One of the first things I prayed after I was saved on July 4, 1972, was that God would give me a way to open the conversation with others. In answer to my prayer, God gave me the idea of taking the icthus, the fish symbol used by early Christians in times of persecution, and superimposing the number seven over it for a lapel pin.

There is seldom a week, often not a day, that goes by that someone doesn't ask me the significance of the pin. I answer that the fish is the symbol of the early Christian; the seven is a reminder that there are seven days in every week and they all belong to Jesus Christ. I explain that I do not worship a part-time Lord, so I do not serve Him on a part-time basis. There is no such thing as a "Sunday

Christian." You either are or you aren't a Christian, and the day of the week has nothing to do with it. Then I ask the person, "Do you know Jesus?" It's an ideal conversation starter, and today thousands of people from all over the world are wearing this "fish and seven" pin.[2]

"May I Share Something with You?"

My friend Dr. Duke Heller from Columbus, Ohio, opens conversations about Jesus by simply asking, "May I share something with you that somebody shared with me?" The answer is invariably yes, and then Duke uses his own unique style of witnessing, pointing out that all of us are sinners, but it's not entirely our fault; that we inherited our sin nature from Adam and all mankind is afflicted with this fatal disease unless we find a solution. Christ, of course, is the solution.

An Invite Card

One of the witnessing tools we in our Sunday school class have found to be effective is a little business card—called an "invite card"—that we hand out as we invite people to visit our class and go to church with us for a great message and beautiful music. When the Redhead and I eat out, time and circumstances permitting, I generally engage the waitperson in conversation. After we've established a rapport, I ask, "Well, the big question is, have you found a church home?" Sometimes the answer is yes; sometimes it's no. I invite them to visit my church as I hand them the business card that gives them the details they'll need if they elect to come visit. Although only about one in ten will fulfill his or her promise to come, some have come to know Christ as a result of that simple invitation.

Let me hasten to say that we should be bold, but not obnoxious, in our witness and we definitely should not interfere with the work a person has to do. Getting an employee in trouble with management will only negate the effectiveness of your witness.

If You're Happy and You
Know It—Show It!

As we share Christ with others, we must be sure to share the joy of the Lord with them. The joy of our salvation has to shine through in order for people to want what we Christians have. Who wants to spend time with people who have gloom and doom written all over their faces? The Bible says that the joy of the Lord is our strength (Nehemiah 8:10)—and *joy, rejoice,* and *rejoicing* are used more than six hundred times in God's Book.

Psalm 32:11 says, "Be glad in the LORD and rejoice, you righteous ones; and shout for joy, all you who are upright in heart." We clap and cheer and shout when our athletic team scores points or wins games. Surely it's more important that genuine joy is reflected in our countenance, our lives, and our witness for Christ.

It's a Package Deal

By far the best way to witness is with your own life as an authentic Christian. We witness to others through the words we say, using the language of love—with no profanity, harshness, anger, or gossip at any time.

The way we dress is also a witness. Josh McDowell says that when we dress in a way that would arouse an appetite we cannot spiritually satisfy, we are guilty of fraud.

We can display the cross and other Christian symbols in the jewelry we wear. We can sign our checks and our correspondence with a Bible verse. In my books, I include a page near the front of each of my books specifically prepared for me to autograph, and when I sign my name, I always include a verse of Scripture—most of the time a salvation verse.

We witness by our participation in church, Sunday school, or

Bible study. We witness in how we treat our spouse, children, parents, siblings, associates, friends, and complete strangers. Not all of us have good persuasion skills, but we should all display the fruit of kindness. And kindness is attractive to many people. It is also a great relationship builder, which is a critical step in successful witnessing.

My friend Dr. James Merritt speaks of "pre-evangelism," meaning that in most cases you need to build a relationship with the person, thereby gaining his or her trust so that your words will have significance to the person to whom you are explaining the gospel.[3]

It Starts at Home

I'm deeply grateful that each of my children, as well as their mates, know and love Christ, so I know that I will spend eternity with them. As Christians, our children need to see the way we treat each other. They need to observe the affection, kindness, and consideration we give one another and the way we respond in daily conversations and interactions. Do they see us praying before each meal? When they see us bow in submission they know we respect authority, and the chances that they will respect our authority as their parents are greatly enhanced.

Children listen to our tone of voice. They observe the way we treat the clerk in the retail store and the wait staff in restaurants. They see how we deal with our neighbors. They listen to our conversations about the people we work with; they notice whether we gossip or whether we follow the Golden Rule.

Our children are aware of when we read our Bible; they notice if we are serious about our prayer life. They know better than anyone else if we faithfully attend worship services, tithe, and support various charities, not only in terms of money, though that can be a factor, but in terms of whether we work with, encourage, and help the underprivileged. I'm not saying that we need to be perfect, of course;

but we should all make a serious effort to be obedient to God's commandments. Do we demonstrate that we really do love the Lord our God with all our heart, soul, and mind, and that we love our neighbors as ourselves? (Matthew 22:37–39).

When these things are observed in our families, the chances are considerably strong that our children will come into the kingdom. There are no guarantees, of course. Children do grow up into adults who must choose or reject Christ, but the chances of them becoming Christians is greatly increased when they see their parents living Christ-filled lives. Being what Christ would have us be in front of our children also prepares us for witnessing in the marketplace and community.

It Flows Over into the Workplace

In the marketplace, our coworkers get a bird's-eye view of exactly what kind of Christians we are. Do we show up for work on time and stay until our commitment for that day is finished? During the lunch breaks, are we careful to stay within the allotted time or do we stretch it into extra time? Do we work as to the Lord, which simply means whether the supervisor or owner is around makes no difference? Are we always effective and motivated in the way we steadily perform our jobs?

Our coworkers are aware of the kind of language we use. When office gossip is going around, do we participate or do we walk away from it? What kind of jokes do we tell or listen to? How do we treat our fellow workers? Are we kind and civil to them? Those of us in a supervisory or management position, do we deal fairly and respectfully with our people? Do we show favoritism or do we deal in a forthright way, regardless of whether the person is friend, family, or the new kid on the block?

There is an old and very true statement that *you teach what you know, but you reproduce what you are.* Not only is this true as we rear our children, but it's also true in the marketplace. We truly are the only Bible that some people will ever read, and we need to make certain they are watching Christians whose only motive is to be pleasing to our heavenly Father if we are going to be of any use to Christ.

What if You Don't Have a Workplace?

What if you are not currently working outside the home? No problem. Your marketplace is where you are. My mother was strong in her faith and possessed a deep compassion and love for others, as well as the conviction that she was supposed to tell folks about Jesus. In the later years of her life, one of my older sisters and her husband, Weldon and Turah Allen, moved in with Mother to take care of her.

Weldon was always with Mother in her beloved garden. She had a great understanding of how to raise peas, tomatoes, butter beans, squash, corn, okra—you name it. She clearly understood what Jesus meant when He said that we would hunger and thirst again, but when we break the bread of life we would never hunger or thirst again (John 6:35).

Weldon Allen loved my mother as much as any of her children did, and he was enormously helpful and encouraging to Mother. While they were working in the garden together, amid all the evidence of God's love, grace, and abundance, my mother shared something even more precious than her love for her own children. She shared Jesus's love for Weldon with him. My mother invited Weldon to get on his knees and surrender his life to Christ, and that's exactly what he did. On those occasions when I thanked Weldon and Turah for taking such good care of my mother, Weldon always made it a point to say that he got a great deal more out of the relationship than my mother ever did. And he was right. Weldon was temporarily very helpful, loving, kind, and considerate to my mother, but my mother, in the marketplace of her life, led him to an eternity with Christ which lasts forever.

Another example of someone who took the gospel into the marketplaces of his life is Colonel Jack Fain. Nobody ever told Colonel Fain about Jesus, but he found Him anyway by reading signs set up alongside the highway like Jesus Is the Way, the Truth and the Life, Jesus Saves, and All Have Sinned and Come Short of the Glory of God. These verses sank into his soul, and one day he got on his knees, confessed his sins, and asked Christ to come into his heart. He participated in revivals and talked about Jesus wherever he went.

Today, at age ninety-three, Colonel Fain is an invalid. Yet he has found a creative way to continue to share his faith with others. He is one of those few people who will never block out his phone number from telemarketers. As a matter of fact, he is thrilled when one calls. He always treats them courteously and graciously, tells them he will listen to everything they have to say but in return they must listen to what he has to say.

Recently, Colonel Fain shared the simple plan of salvation and led a telemarketer to a saving knowledge of Christ. The caller hung up rejoicing, and Colonel Fain felt an unspeakable joy that is unequaled by anything else we can experience on planet earth.

Colonel Fain's example of being obedient and available eliminates any so-called legitimate excuses any of us think we have for not using our resources to tell the greatest story ever told. Christ does not call us to be perfect, but He does call us to speak up and speak out—and that includes telling people next door and those who call us on the phone about Jesus. So, as you can see, having a place to go to work is not necessary for us to reach out with the good news. The marketplace is wherever you and one other person make contact.

INTO THE MARKETPLACE YOU GO

It is impossible to even imagine the eternal blessing that comes when you are faithful to share your faith in Christ and God uses the occasion to bring someone into the kingdom. When you get to the goal line of life and look into eternity, wouldn't it be wonderful to see your children, friends, relatives, grandchildren, and great-grand-children, who are now going to spend eternity with you because at some point in your life you led someone to Christ who led someone to Christ who led someone to Christ, until indirectly you have led one of your own great-grandchildren to the Lord? We never know the extent to which God will take our faithfulness and bring about miraculous results.

In the Great Commission, Jesus tells us, "Go." Prayerfully go into your marketplace. Tell all who will listen that Jesus is the Way, the Truth, and the Life and that none come to the Father except by Him (John 14:6).

Tell somebody today that *God's way is still the best way*!

APPENDIX
Why Must We Be Born Again?

The Bible reveals that human beings are in a condition of spiritual death because of sin and unrighteousness. Dead things cannot fellowship with living things. Everything in God's kingdom is alive. To be in God's kingdom, human beings must have life also. That life is found by faith in Jesus Christ.

Jesus is God's means and provision to transform us from a condition of spiritual death to spiritual life. Jesus said, "I am the way, and the truth, and the life; no one comes to the Father but through Me" (John 14:6).

God's terms for people to receive new life are for us to lay down our rebellion against Him, repent, and recognize that Jesus is the source of the life we need, and to receive that life by faith. We cannot simply clean up our old life; we need a completely new and transformed life—we need to be *born again*. This is the truth revealed in Scripture.

Therefore, people who are not born again—transformed by the saving grace of Jesus Christ—are not really Christians. They remain in spiritual death. They may be a Christian philosopher and try to support the teachings of Jesus, but unless they commit their lives to the Lord and receive His new and eternal life by faith, they remain in death.

Maybe the discussion Nicodemus had with Jesus will help clarify some of this.

> Now there was a man of the Pharisees, named Nicodemus, a
> ruler of the Jews; this man came to Jesus by night and said to Him,

"Rabbi, we know that You have come from God as a teacher; for no one can do these signs that You do unless God is with him."

Jesus answered and said to him, "Truly, truly, I say to you, unless one is born again he cannot see the kingdom of God."

Nicodemus said to Him, "How can a man be born when he is old? He cannot enter a second time into his mother's womb and be born, can he?"

Jesus answered, "Truly, truly, I say to you, unless one is born of water and the Spirit he cannot enter into the kingdom of God. That which is born of the flesh is flesh, and that which is born of the Spirit is spirit. Do not be amazed that I said to you, 'You must be born again.'" . . .

"For God so loved the world, that He gave His only begotten Son, that whoever believes in Him shall not perish, but have eternal life. For God did not send the Son into the world to judge the world, but that the world might be saved through Him. He who believes in Him is not judged; he who does not believe has been judged already, because he has not believed in the name of the only begotten Son of God. This is the judgment, that the Light has come into the world, and men loved the darkness rather than the Light, for their deeds were evil. For everyone who does evil hates the Light, and does not come to the Light for fear that his deeds will be exposed. But he who practices the truth comes to the Light, so that his deeds may be manifested as having been wrought in God." (John 3:1-7, 16–21)

If you still have questions about being "born again," please feel free to e-mail me at lmagers@ziglar.com or write me at:

Ziglar
15303 Dallas Parkway, Suite 550
Addison, TX 75001

ACKNOWLEDGMENTS

As always when I write a book, I require a lot of direct and indirect help. Everything starts with the process I follow, which is to dictate what I want in print. Laurie Magers, my executive assistant for more than thirty years, transcribes the dictation into computer files.

My youngest daughter, Julie Norman, edits my books, and she and Laurie work together beautifully. Julie has stored every example and story I've used in previous books, which helps me to avoid too much repetition. Julie and Laurie correspond often, and their counsel has been invaluable over the years.

The real heroes of this book are the men and women who set the examples I have found to be personally helpful. There are so many I can't possibly name them all, but to them I am eternally grateful. My good friend Jeff Nyberg, a former pastor of the Sunday school class I taught, has been a particularly helpful theological resource. He still visits me personally as well as corresponding by phone, fax, and e-mail when I can't come up with the answers I'm looking for. His willingness to respond and to point me toward helpful resources is invaluable.

Our senior pastor at Prestonwood Baptist Church, Dr. Jack Graham, gives me confidence every Sunday when he *preaches* the Bible and does not *debate* it. His messages are powerful and informative, consistently resulting in numerous people committing their lives to Christ. His friend and teaching pastor, Dr. David McKinley, has also contributed a great deal through his lessons and willingness to answer my questions, of which there have been many.

Other pastors and Bible students who have been very helpful to me in this effort include Dr. Ike Reighard, Dr. James Merritt, Dr. Paige Patterson, Dr. Tim Timmons, and my friend, Rabbi Daniel Lapin.

Dr. Frank Minirth, of the nationally respected Minirth Clinic in Dallas, responded to my calls often to validate information, which I do from psychological, theological, and physiological standpoints before I write, record, or verbalize it.

The editorial help I received from Joey Paul, Jennifer Stair, and Kris Bearss has been invaluable. I'm grateful that Thomas Nelson made such talented people available to work with me on this book.

Those of you who have read my books before know that I rely heavily on the insight and considerable knowledge of my bride of sixty-plus years. When I'm talking about her, I call her the Redhead. When I'm talking to her, I call her Sugar Baby. But her name is Jean. She readily takes on the responsibility of the daily things that are critically important, many of which I don't like to do at all and so, consequently, do them poorly. She gives me complete freedom to write, study, and teach. Her insight, love, support, and encouragement have been the driving force in my life and make it easy for me to do what I do best. Her love is constant and her support is unfailing—just some of the reasons that after sixty years of marriage, we are more in love than ever. She is the biggest blessing in my life, and I am eternally grateful to God for bestowing her on me.

NOTES

FOREWORD

1. Zig Ziglar, *See You at the Top* (Gretna, LA: Pelican, reprint 1982).

INTRODUCTION

1. Ed Silvoso, *Anointed for Business* (New York: Regal, 2006).

CHAPTER 1: LOVE

1. http://www.chick-fil-a.com/WinShapeFacts.asp.
2. For more on John Eagan's story, see Lois Trigg Chaplin, *The Golden Rule at Work Since 1905* (Birmingham, AL: American Cast Iron Pipe Company, 2005).

CHAPTER 2: JOY

1. *Brian Buffini, Oh, By the Way . . . : A Wonderful Way to Sell and Be Sold To* (Carlsbad, CA: Olivemount, 2002).
2. Brian Buffini, "Seven Biblical Principles of the Referral Process," *Turning Point Workbook* (self-published, 1995). Used by permission.

CHAPTER 3: PEACE

1. Used by permission of Dr. Dick Furman.
2. You can read more about Wayne Alderson and his experience at Pittron Steel in *Stronger Than Steel: The Wayne Alderson Story* by R. C. Sproul (New York: Harper and Row, 1999), as well as *Theory R Management*, a book penned by Alderson and his daughter, Nancy Alderson McDonnell (Nashville: Thomas Nelson, 1994). To order these books or

to get more information about Wayne Alderson's Value of The Person-Theory R Business Seminars, go to www.valueoftheperson.com.

3. Peter Grazier, "The Miracle of Pittron Steel," http://www.teambuilding.com/article_valuing_people.htm.

CHAPTER 4: PATIENCE

1. http://www.usatoday.com/sports/preps/football/2003-09-10-mckissick-milestone_x.htm.

2. Ibid.

3. From the personal files of John McKissick. Used with permission.

4. Quoted in Jill Lieber, "Football coach all alone at brink of 500 wins: Nobody at any level has won as much as high school legend," *USA Today,* September 11, 2003, C.01.

5. William McKenzie, "White evangelicals, black churches could reshape politics," *Dallas Morning News,* November 9, 2003.

6. Candi Cushman, "Showing the Alternative: Changed Hearts," *World* Magazine, 21 April 2001.

7. McKenzie, "White evangelicals, black churches could reshape politics," November 9, 2003.

8. Ibid.

9. For more information, see Susan Everly-Douze, "Zebco Meets the Challenges of Fish-Eat-Fish Competition," *Tulsa World,* April 26, 1992.

CHAPTER 5: KINDNESS

1. Noah Webster, *American Dictionary of the English Language,* 7th ed. (Springfield, MA: G & C Merriam Company, 1993), s.v. "kindness."

2. For more information on this research, see http://www3.baylor.edu/hhtr/curves.

CHAPTER 6: GOODNESS

1. Mike Lopresti, "Times Have Changed for the Once-Shunned Miami," *USA Today*, 21 May 2003.

CHAPTER 10: AN INTIMATE RELATIONSHIP

1. Barna Research Group, "Americans are most likely to base truth on feelings," Barna.org, February 12, 2002.

CHAPTER 11: SHARING CHRIST WITH OTHERS

1. Charles Spurgeon, quoted in *Revoluzion*, September 2006; revoluzion247.blogspot.com/2006_09_01_archive.html.
2. If you are interested in using the fish and seven pin in your personal witness, through your church or denomination, go to our Web site (www.ziglar.com) or e-mail us for information (info@ziglar.com). Purchase one or more for your personal use, or if you would like to use it as an evangelical tool for your ministry and want to purchase several of them, we will provide you contact information so you can order directly from the manufacturer.
3. Dr. James Merritt, *Religion & Ethics Newsweekly*, April 26, 2002, Episode #534.

ABOUT THE AUTHOR

ZIG ZIGLAR is an internationally known author and speaker whose client list includes thousands of businesses, Fortune 500 companies, US government agencies, churches, schools, and nonprofit associations. Many of his twenty-six books have been bestsellers, including *See You at the Top, Raising Positive Kids in a Negative World,* and *Secrets of Closing the Sale.* Ziglar is also chairman of the Zig Ziglar Corporation and Ziglar, Inc., which help people more fully utilize their physical, mental, and spiritual resources. He and his wife, "the Redhead," live in Texas.

GOD'S WAY IS STILL THE BEST WAY
Let Zig help you share that good news!

Zig Ziglar has written three popular tracts to help you express how God's way is always best.

I BELIEVE IN CHRISTMAS

The politically correct "Happy holidays!" greeting prompted Zig to respond with a clear Christmas message. This tract is perfect to share the real reason for the Christmas season with anyone.

I KNOW YOU ARE HURTING

Zig shares the pain he felt when his grown daughter died, yet even in that painful experience he learned that "Our loving Heavenly Father will always act in the long-range best interests of his children."

WILL I SEE YOU AT THE TOP?

It's important that we make it to the top—not the top of a corporate or religious ladder, but all the way to God. Jesus makes this possible for us, and Zig tells how.

God's way is the best way! Let Zig help you share that with those around you:
Write **Good News Publishers, 1300 Crescent Street, Wheaton, IL 60187**
Order securely online at **www.goodnewstracts.org** or order toll-free at **877.872.2871**

God's Way TRULY Is Still the Best Way

Many organizations find themselves looking for ways to gain a competitive advantage in today's fast paced and technology driven business world. Some are even willing to get very close to the line or maybe even cross the line, ultimately compromising their character in an attempt to win. We believe that you can do more than just win in business, you can win in all aspects of your personal and professional life, and most importantly your spiritual life. Give us a call today to learn more about introducing Ziglar training programs into your culture and organization. Zig's time tested and proven principles have helped thousands of individuals and hundreds of companies over the years meet and exceed their goals while at the same time adhering to the very foundational principles found within this book, *God's Way Is Still the Best Way*.

Learn to **sell** with **integrity, present** with **passion, assure customer loyalty** through **trust,** and how to develop a culture of character within your organization.

Call us today at 1.800.527.0306 or visit us at www.ziglar.com.

To learn more about classic Zig programs such as *Christian Motivation for Daily Living* and *Raising Positive Kids in a Negative World* visit our website or call and speak to one of our friendly, professional performance representatives; <u>mention this book</u> when you call and **receive a FREE 10 day subscription to the NEW Ziglar Vault.**

You are not alone
on your
grief journey

Some tear-stained steps
will be painful...
some confusing...

May God comfort
your
Grieving Heart

We find comfort in remembering
our loved one is in heaven,
but we ache for the void left in our lives,
especially during a holiday
– Zig Ziglar

With Heartfelt
Sympathy

As valuable as the words of loved ones
are to us through our grief,
no words are more
powerful than God's.
– Zig Ziglar

Zig Ziglar's Voices of Comfort

greeting cards are eloquently written with a graceful touch especially for those who are grieving. Each card message is adapted from Zig's best-selling book, **"Confessions of a Grieving Christian"**. *It is Zig's hope that the cards extend his voice and God's love to the hurting.*

Visit your local Christian bookstore to purchase one of Zig's sympathy cards endorsed by internationally recognized GriefShare. This organization provides ongoing encouragement and help to grieving people on the road to recovery. Zig is one of 48 acclaimed Christians featured on the GriefShare video seminars. To find a GriefShare group near you, visit www.GriefShare.org . To preview the entire Zig Ziglar greeting card line, please visit www.dicksonsgifts.com

Grief brings moments of sorrow, but the Lord sends moments of comfort that overcome the sorrow.
-Zig Ziglar

DICKSONS
800.457.9885

With Heartfelt
Sympathy

Zig Ziglar Center
For Ethical Leadership
at Southern Nazarene University

IN OKLAHOMA CITY, OKLAHOMA

This book would not be complete if I didn't tell you about the most exciting thing happening in the field of ethical leadership to date. Much of the material you've just read and more like it will be upgraded, expanded and taught at the university level. Finally, an institution of higher learning is going to teach people how to live a life on higher ground.

I am so honored and excited to be working with Southern Nazarene University. This university shares my passion for creating high quality, ethical leaders. Our hearts and minds are one in our efforts to create an educational partnership that will influence our future leaders to be moral, ethical, and service oriented in their faith-based business practices.

For the first time a PhD program in ethical leadership is being offered at SNU. I have complete faith in the university's ability to teach and uphold the principles I've long taught because God is at the core of all SNU curriculum. The Center's mission statement reads: The mission of the Zig Ziglar Center for Ethical Leadership at Southern Nazarene University is to promote leadership development, character formation, ethical business practice and positive, faith-based life skills.

To learn more about how you can help make a difference in the lives of our future leaders please visit www.snu.edu/ziglar.